South Lakeland Walks with Children

Nick Lambert

Published by Sigma Leisure – an imprint of
Sigma Press, 5 Alton Road, Wilmslow, Cheshire SK9 5DY, England.

British Library Cataloguing in Publication Data

A CIP record for this book is available from the British Library.

ISBN: 978-1-85058-578-7

Typesetting and Design by: Sigma Press, Wilmslow, Cheshire.

Cover photograph: Waterhead, Coniston Water *(Nick Lambert)*

Maps and photographs: Nick Lambert

Printed by: Progress Press Ltd, Malta

Disclaimer: the information in this book is given in good faith and is believed to be correct at the time of publication. No responsibility is accepted by either the author or publisher for errors or omissions, or for any loss or injury howsoever caused. Only you can judge your own fitness, competence and experience.

Preface

The Lake District needs little introduction. Tucked up there in the north-west of England it boasts the highest mountain in England, the most climbed mountain, the longest lake and alas, the most rain, but that last one shouldn't be taken too seriously.

It is an area known for its mountains, but there are plenty of 'training peaks' for families embarking on their first walking adventure together, and some spectacular scenery in the many valleys. Most of the twenty walks in this book have escape routes, so you can tailor the length to suit your time or energy.

All route directions have been thoroughly checked and re-checked, but each time I have been surprised to see many quite drastic changes, including paths being reworked, re-routed, stiles and gates being interchanged, or collapsing altogether. In short, the walks were accurate at the time this book was written, but changes do occur, so please carry the appropriate maps with you, in case you lose your way.

Finally, take care on the fells, respect the countryside and enjoy your walking in Lakeland.

Nick Lambert

Contents

Before you Begin . . .   **1**
Introductory notes on the text   1
Sketch maps   1
Quick Reference Chart   2
The Country Code *(and other commonsense advice)*   3
A Note About Public Rights of Way   4
Tourist Information Centres   4

The Walks

1. Broughton Moor   **5**
Distance: *2½ miles*

2. Coniston Water - Western Shore   **11**
Distance: *2 miles (return via ferry)*

3. Cunswick Scar   **19**
Distance: *3 miles or 6 miles.*

4. Easedale   **29**
Distance: *4½ miles*

5. Elterwater & the Forces and Little Langdale   **39**
Distance: *4 miles or 6 miles.*

6. Eskdale   **54**
Distance: *3½ miles*

7. Finsthwaite   **63**
Distance: *2 miles*

8. Grasmere and Rydal Water   **71**
Distance: *3 miles, 3½ miles or 5½ miles*

9. Great Langdale   **79**

Distance: *4 miles*

10. Grizedale   **86**

Distance: *5 miles*

11. Hawkshead & Latterbarrow   **95**

Distance: *4 miles*

12. Kentmere   **106**

Distance: *6 miles*

13. Near Sawrey   **116**

Distance: *2 miles*

14. Orrest Head   **123**

Distance: *2 miles*

15. Ravenglass & Muncaster   **133**

Distance: *4½ miles*

16. Tarn Hows   **142**

Distance: *2 miles or 3 miles*

17. Todd Crag   **150**

Distance: *2 miles*

18. Wasdale Head   **157**

Distance: *3 miles*

19. Wastwater & Nether Wasdale   **164**

Distance: *3½ miles*

20. Witherslack   **171**

Distance: *3 miles*

50 Questions & Answers for Boring Journeys   **181**

Ideas for Games on Long Journeys   **185**

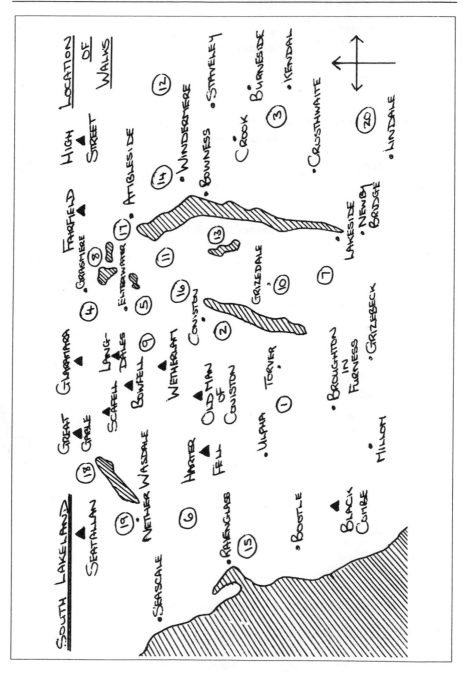

Before you Begin . . .

Introductory notes on the text

This is a very unusual book, intended to be read by both parents and children. The following conventions have been used to make the book as useful as possible to both categories:

1. **Directions are numbered and appear in bold text so that they can be seen at a glance.**

☺ Information for the children is set in a contrasting typestyle. This is to be read aloud, or for them to read themselves. **OTHER INFORMATION FOR PARENTS APPEARS IN BOLD CAPITALS.**

Questions (and answers) are in the same type style, with "Q" and "A".

In between the instructions you will often see text that looks like this. We have used this for all sorts of extra information, ranging from background material to escape routes – generally, the sort of thing you can skate over if you are in a rush to complete the main walk.

Checklists appear at the end of each walk, for the children to tick off things as they see them. If you do not want to write in the book, copy the checklist onto a piece of paper, and give one to each child, so that they can compete to see who spots the most.

Sketch maps

The maps are intended only as a rough guide to the route and are not drawn to scale. Unless otherwise stated north is upwards. Only buildings important to the route are shown. Numbers refer to the directions given in the text.

Roads   =   a continuous line
Footpaths   =   a dotted line
Trackways/forest roads/driveways   =   a line of dashes
Parking   =   P
Public house   =   PH

Quick Reference Chart

The index chart allows you to plan your day at a glance, to check each route has the features or facilities you require. For more information on these see the individual route.

Notes & Key
Pushchairs: Walks with at least a small route suitable for pushchairs, though it may involve some effort.
Bus: Routes that are within a short walk from a bus stop.
Café: A café or tearoom along the route or within easy walking distance.
Pubs: A pub along the route where families are welcome, with seats outside or a family room.
Flat: The route is more or less flat, or can be made flat using escape routes.
Historical: A place of historical interest features along the route, or close by.
Features: Places of specific interest to children along the route or close by.

	Pushchairs	Rail	Bus	Café	Pubs	Flat	Historical	Features
1. Broughton Moor								Sea views
2. Coniston Water	*		*	*	*	*	*	Boat trips
3. Cunswick Scar								Wildlife/Views
4. Easedale			*	*	*		*	Playground
5. Elterwater			*	*	*			
6. Eskdale		*	*	*	*		*	Miniature Railway
7. Finsthwaite			*	*	*		*	Steam Railway
8. Grasmere			*	*	*		*	Tourist Hotspot
9. Great Langdale			*	*	*			
10. Grizedale	*		*	*		**	*	Playground
11. Hawkshead			*	*	*		*	Tourist Hotspot
12. Kentmere			*				*	
13. Near Sawrey			*	*	*		*	Hill Top (NT)
14. Orrest Head		*	*	*	*			Viewpoint
15. Ravenglass		*	*	*	*		*	Trains/Playground
16. Tarn Hows	*				*			Lake Views
17. Todd Crag			*	*	*			Playground
18. Wasdale Head				*	*			
19. Wastwater					*			
20. Witherslack			*		*			Wildlife

The Country Code
(and other commonsense advice)

☆ Don't drop litter. If there is no bin, take it home with you.

☆ The countryside should be a place of peace and tranquillity. Do not ruin it for other people by shouting and screaming.

☆ Close all gates after you, otherwise you might cause flocks of sheep to stray onto the road and get run over.

☆ Keep dogs on leads when there are farm animals around, and keep them under close control at all times.

☆ Do not try to get too near to wild animals, as many of them will be frightened and may *bite*!

☆ If stroking farm animals such as horses, keep fingers *well away* from their mouths, or you may lose them.

☆ Always stick to the public footpaths/bridleways, and do not stray onto private land.

☆ Some farms use electric fences to separate fields. These are usually a single wire held up by occasional plastic supports. The voltage is low, and won't kill you. Even so, it's not a good idea to grab hold of them, as a shock can be alarming.

☆ Do not cross railway lines, except by proper crossing places, such as bridges.

☆ Always walk on the right-hand side of a lane or road, so that you are walking *towards* the traffic, so that you can see any approaching vehicle. Keep well into the side of the road and keep in single file. Restrain small children as traffic approaches.

☆ Do not pick wild flowers. Leave them for others to enjoy.

☆ Never eat wild berries. They may look colourful and tasty, like sweets, but many are deadly poisonous. The same goes for mushrooms and toadstools. No matter how nice and colourful they look, don't touch them.

☆ Never fool around near water. Do not paddle in a stream or pond unless an adult says it is safe to do so.

☆ Respect the countryside and enjoy your walk!

A Note About Public Rights of Way

In many areas there are a lot of problems with farmers and landowners illegally blocking public footpaths. The Lake District, being a National Park, thankfully has very few such problems. Two of the rare exceptions encountered while writing this book were on National Trust land, of all places, and while the paths were not blocked, the NT seem to be trying to pretend they do not exist by keeping them unsigned and not showing them on their maps. I'm still trying to find out why, and they are still trying not to let on.

Public footpaths are, in most cases, ancient rights of way, and not even the landowner has the right to prevent their use. If you encounter hazards or blocked paths on your walk, then the Ramblers' Association would like to hear from you. Always double check the correct route of the right of way on an up-to-date Ordnance Survey map. The address of the RA head office is:

The Ramblers' Association
Wandsworth Road
London SW8 2XX

Tourist Information Centres

For information on opening times, buses, trains, places to stay and practically anything else, try the T.I.C. They are usually very helpful and know everything you could possibly want to know about the Lake District. The telephone numbers of some of the main ones are listed below:

Ambleside: 015394-32582

Bowness-on-Windermere: 015394-42895

Coniston: 015394-41533

Egremont: 01946-820693

Grasmere: 015394-35245

Hawkshead: 015394-36525

Kendal: 01539-725758

1. Broughton Moor

This is a seldom-visited area within the National Park. A quiet forest, ideal for times during school holidays when the rest of Lakeland is heaving with people.

Starting point: Any of the car parks or layby on Hummer Lane, along the southern edge of the forest. From Torver follow the A593 south-west for 1 mile, then bear right up the steep winding lane. After a further mile you should arrive at Broughton Moor forest. The main car park is signed at the beginning of the forest as being 600 metres ahead. (SD252927)

Distance: 2½ miles

Terrain: Forest trackways, grassy footpaths and a quiet lane. Some uphill stretches, but nothing too severe. May be muddy in parts.

Maps: OS Leisure 6, OS Landranger 96

Public Toilets: None

Refreshments: None in the vicinity

1. **From the car park bear left, heading back along the lane.**

☺ Along the sides of this quiet lane there are grassy banks with ferns and heather growing on them. Heather is a low plant that grows well in bad weather conditions, in places where there might be a lot of strong wind, such as hilltops and moors like this. It has very small purple flowers and dark green leaves.

On the right there are fields which may have sheep or cows in them, and looking back, into the distance, you should be able to see the sea.

2. **Some way along the lane you should come to a sign on the left: 'Forest Enterprise, Broughton Moor, Parking 600m'. Follow the trackway that leads off to the left at this point, signed as a public bridleway. Go through the gate and continue ahead, downhill.**

☺ Close to the gate there is a post with a sign warning about the dangers of fire. Hanging from the post are several strange looking objects, which are fire-beaters, for putting out any fires

Broughton Moor Forest

that start. In dry weather there is a great danger of fire in a forest like this. Fires can easily start by careless people dropping cigarette ends or lighting small fires that soon get out of control, or by the sun reflecting on broken glass.

Q: What number would you dial on a telephone to get through to the Fire Brigade?

A: 999. The same number for the police or an ambulance.

☺ Over on the right you may be able to see Broughton Moor Slate Quarry, where slate is cut from the hillside. The left of the trackway is a small, disused quarry. Can you recognise it?

3. Continue along the main trackway as it winds downhill and levels out at the bottom. Avoid the minor footpath off to the right.

☺ On the left of the track there is a high grassy bank, with many new trees planted on it. They may be in plastic protectors to keep them safe from wild animals that might gnaw at the soft bark and damage the tree.

☺ Amongst the trees there are many tall plants with purple bell-like

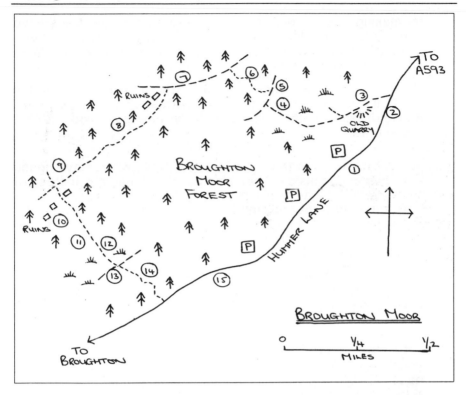

flowers in the summer. These are called foxgloves. Another tall plant that can be found all over the forest, also with purple flowers, is the thistle, which has sharp prickles to protect it.

In the summer you may hear grasshoppers in the grass. They make a sort of humming sound. They are often difficult to see, as they tend to blend well with leaves and bark, so they are 'camouflaged'. Grasshoppers get their name from their ability to jump great distances. They can 'hop' up to twenty times their own length. They bury their eggs in the ground throughout the summer, and they will hatch in the next spring, when the weather gets warmer.

4. **The track soon bears around to the right to a junction. Keep to the main trackway to the right, avoiding the grassy track bearing off to the left through the trees.**

☺ Look out for yellow signs warning of tree felling in progress. The trees are cut down for their wood, which is used for building and for making paper. You may see tree stumps, where trees have been felled. Also look out for areas of trees that have been planted so that there is always a steady supply of wood available. It takes twenty or thirty years for the trees to become fully grown.

5. **The track leads very slightly uphill. After a short way take the small footpath off to the left, signed with an arrow, which leads downhill between the undergrowth, becoming a clear path between trees.**

☺ Most of the trees in the forest are 'conifers', which have cones with their seeds inside. They also have dark needles instead of flat leaves. They are quicker growing than many other types of tree, and their trunks are tall and straight, so they can easily be sawn into planks. There are many different types of conifer, and they all have very different cones. Look on the ground and see how many different types of cone you can find.

6. **Follow the path (occasionally signed) as it winds downhill between the trees. At the bottom it joins a trackway. Bear left, still leading slightly downhill.**

☺ A small stream soon joins the path on the left. This is called a 'tributary' because it joins a larger stream, which is just up ahead. This larger stream in turn joins the River Lickle, which joins the River Duddon and then empties into the sea.

7. **The track crosses over the main stream via a concrete bridge. Bear left immediately after the bridge.**

(At this point there are many shallow pools suitable for paddling.)

☺ See if you can spot the floors of some buildings on the right of the path, which have now been demolished. Also see if you can see any nesting boxes in the trees, which are put there to encourage certain small birds to nest in the forest.

8. **Follow the path ahead with the stream over on your left. It is quite a narrow but clear path.**

☺ There are several 'gorse' bushes along the path. They have yellow flowers in the summer, and very sharp prickles. After a short way the path becomes sheltered by overhanging trees, and soon comes close to the beck again. Many small streams cross the path and join the beck.

Soon the path climbs above the stream, and if you look down at this point you should be able to see, and hear, a waterfall, where the beck is forced through a gap in the rock.

After the waterfall the path drops down again and you should be able to see the ruins of some stone buildings on the opposite side of the water.

9. **Cross the stream via the stepping stones and follow the narrow winding grassy path between the ruins, with your back to the stream.**

☺ As you can see, the roofs of these old buildings have long since fallen in and many of the walls are partly collapsed. The insides are now overgrown with nettles and blackberry bushes. Can you make out where there were once doorways and windows? Never play in or climb on ruins like these, because you can never be sure they are safe, and the walls might come down on top of you.

10. **Continue straight ahead along the path, which starts to lead uphill between conifers. There are occasional white marks on trees to show the way.**

☺ Some trees have fallen over and you can see their roots sticking up into the air. Tree roots do not usually go down very deeply into the ground, but they spread out for a long way in all directions. They collect water from the ground and feed the tree.

11. **After the trees keep straight ahead across the open grassy area. There are now occasional white topped posts to show the way.**

☺ This path might be marshy in places, so watch where you put your feet. Look out for an old tree stump which has been carved into arrows to point the direction of the path.

Over on the right there are views downhill over the rest of the forest.

12. **The path leads into a further area of trees. Again there are white marks on the trees to show the way.**

13. **At the end of the trees cross the forest trackway and continue ahead, almost opposite, along a grassy path leading between young conifers. Again follow the occasional white topped posts.**

Q: The Path winds between bracken, gorse, thistles and

blackberries. Which of these four plants does NOT have prickles?

A: Bracken is a type of fern, and it does not have prickles. It is also the only one of the four plants which does not have a flower.

☺ Look out for rabbits running for cover in the undergrowth.

14. **The path winds for some way. When you reach the stile cross over and bear left alongside the road. (Grass banks and verges on both sides.)**

☺ Again there are views down to the sea. Perhaps you can see a lighthouse on the coast, warning ships that they are getting close to the land.

At certain points there are views to the left between the trees over the forest through which you have walked.

15. **Continue ahead along the road to the car park/s.**

Broughton Moor Checklist

☐ A fallen tree

☐ A lighthouse

☐ A purple flower

☐ A white flower

☐ A fir cone

☐ A plant with prickles

☐ A sheep

☐ A squirrel

☐ A wooden gate

☐ A birds nest

☐ A robin

☐ A plane

☐ A nettle

☐ A tree stump

2. Coniston Water - Western Shore

One of the best ways to enjoy Coniston Water is by foot and ferry. The ferries run approximately every hour between March and November, but check with local tourist information or at the landing stage close to the Lake Road car park. This is the lake on which most of Arthur Ransome's 'Swallows and Amazons' is set, and was also used as the location for the film of the book.

Starting Point: The Bluebird Café, at the end of Lake Road, Coniston. Signed in the village for the lake & launches. There is a car-park just next to the café.

By bus: The 'Coniston Rambler' service, from Bowness via Ambleside

Distance: 2 miles (return via ferry)

Terrain: Completely flat! Good gravelled paths for most of the way.

Maps: OS Landranger 96 or 97, OS Outdoor Leisure 6 or 7

Public Toilets: At the Bluebird Café

Refreshments: The Bluebird Café

Pushchairs: This route is entirely flat, so with a bit (quite a bit) of effort it can be done with pushchairs. The paths are mainly gravelled, but not all of them are, and there are a couple of stiles to negotiate.

☺ **(AT THE BEACH.)** This is Coniston Water, which, as you should be able to tell, is a popular place to come boating or windsurfing. There are often ducks and geese on the beach, on the look-out for food.

(Check on the pier for the times of the Coniston Launch, so you can adjust your walk accordingly. The launch travels in a figure of eight, so the return journey from Torver to Coniston will also call at Brantwood on the opposite shore.)

1. **Return along Lake Road, heading away from the water. There is a path alongside the stream in places, winding between the trees.**

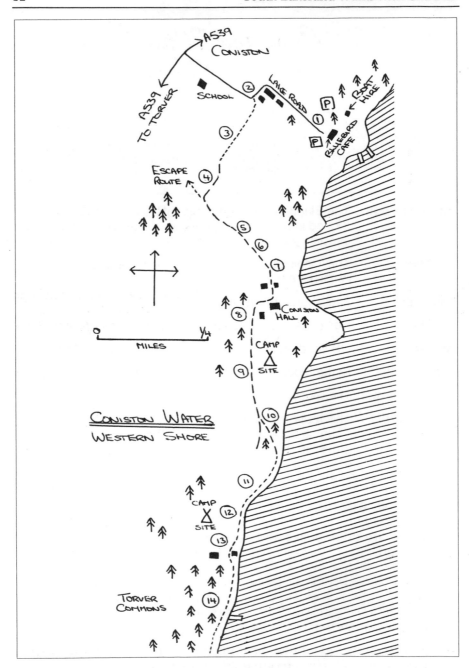

☺ The stream on your left is called Church Beck, and it passes close to the church in the heart of the village of Coniston, carrying water down from the high fells, into the lake. It is quite wide at this point, and if you look into the water you will see it is very clear, and there are stones on the bottom, many of which are slate.

Coniston came into being as a mining village, but today it is popular with tourists, who come to enjoy the lake and the surrounding countryside. Walkers flock here to climb some of the high surrounding fells, especially the Coniston Old Man, which is the highest fell in the area.

Q: Soon you will cross over an arched stone bridge. The stone is slate which is quarried close by. What does it say on the slate plaque in the middle of the bridge?

A: Lake Road.

2. **After the bridge pass the driveway to the Lake Road workshops on the left, and take the wooden gate or stile at the corner as the road bears sharply to the right and heads towards Coniston. Bear right along the edge of the field.**

☺ There are often cows or sheep in this field. Keep a look out on the grass for strands of wool.

Q: What do cows and sheep eat?

A: Everyone should know that one! They eat grass mainly, or any other plants that happen to be around.

3. **At the end of the field go through the gate on the right and follow the gravelled trackway around to the left.**

☺ Over on the right you can see the Coniston fells in the background, with their bare rocky tops. Below there are rows of houses rising up, many of them built of slate.

The path is now heading towards some woods, made up mainly of deciduous trees, which means that they lose their leaves in the winter. In the autumn they are very colourful, as the leaves begin to turn yellow, brown or red.

4. **After a short way follow the main trackway as it bears around to the left, avoiding the minor path leading off to the right.**

Escape Route (for Coniston village): bear right along the minor path and follow it as it leads up to the road. Bear right for the village centre.

☺ As you follow the trackway, you should soon be able to see the distinctive tall, round chimneys of Coniston Hall, rising ahead above the treetops. This is the oldest building in the area, many hundreds of years old. It once belonged to a wealthy family, but today it is owned by the National Trust, who now own much of the National Park.

Q: If you look around you, you should be able to see a church. Does it have a tower or a spire?

A: A tower.

☺ Above the church is the Coniston Old Man, which might be hidden in mist if the weather is bad. From the top, on a clear day, you can see as far as Blackpool Tower. You should be able to make out heaps of abandoned slate on the Old Man, left over from the quarrying and copper mines.

5. **The track soon crosses a stream via a bridge, after which go through the gate and continue ahead.**

☺ The stream runs down from the slopes behind the church and empties into the lake, which you should be able to see between the trees on the left. There will probably be many boats moored close to the bank.

Coniston Water is a long, straight lake, and was used in 1967 by Donald Campbell, who was trying to beat the World Water Speed Record. His boat reached an amazing 300 miles per hour, before it flipped over and exploded, killing him. The café close to the car park at the start of the walk is named after his boat, 'Bluebird'.

6. **Continue ahead, joining a driveway, and bearing left towards the hall.**

Q: You should now have a clear view of the hall. How many chimneys are there?

A: There are 5 in all: 4 are tall, round and white, but there is another shorter stone chimney as well.

7. **Follow the driveway as it bears right in front of the hall. Go**

through the gateway (often open) and continue ahead, keeping with the main driveway as it leads through the trees.

☺ There are sometimes hens and peacocks running around here. Peacocks are male, the females are 'peahens'. The male bird has long, colourful tail feathers which he can fan out behind him if he feels like showing off.

Q: Soon there should be a fenced area of woodland on the right. Can you recognise any of the trees? There are hawthorn, birch, elder and oak. Which of these trees do you think have berries?

A: Hawthorn and elder both have berries. The fruit of the oak tree is, of course, the acorn, while the fruit of the birch is called a 'catkin'.

8. **Keep with the main concrete driveway as it passes through a gateway (again, often open) onto the campsite. Continue ahead, taking care to avoid trackways leading off on either side.**

☺ Throughout the summer this is a popular campsite, where you might see tents or caravans. Perhaps you have been on a camping trip with school, or perhaps you are staying in a tent at the moment. Camping can be a lot of fun, but it can also be very cold in the mornings!

9. **After some way the main drive bears left nearer to the lake. At this point look out for a gravel trackway leading further off to the left, signed with a yellow arrow. Follow this between fenced areas of trees. Continue along the track, with the lake now on your left.**

☺ Some of the trees in the fenced area alongside the path have red berries which ripen in the autumn. The trees are called 'whitebeams', and they have clusters of white flowers in the spring. Look out also for 'conifers', which have cones and needles instead of leaves.

10. **Follow the path and go through the gate in the drystone wall. Continue ahead along the shoreline.**

☺ You should now have a clear view across the lake. Most of the opposite shore is covered with trees. This is part of Grizedale Forest, which spreads for several miles. The trees nearest to the lake are deciduous, and look very colourful in the autumn. Higher up the trees are mainly conifers.

The large white house is called 'Brantwood' (which means 'steep wood'). It was once the home of John Ruskin, who was a famous artist and poet. Perhaps you can make out the 'turret' window at the front of the house, which looks a bit like the top of a lighthouse. He had this special window built onto his bedroom so he could sit and look out over the lake in almost every direction. He spent hours just watching the surface of the water and the clouds and the boats.

Today there are many different types of boat on the lake. One of them is called 'Gondola' and is an old steam yacht which has been repaired to working order. It sails up and down the lake taking passengers. See if you can see it. Also there are many different ferries, which can carry a lot of people at once. Then there are small rowing boats which can carry a few people, and canoes for only one person.

Along the edge of the lake there are occasional hawthorn bushes and oak trees. Notice how the roots close to the lake have been uncovered by the high winter tides, which have washed the shale away.

Towards the end of the field there are good views from the waters

The 'Gondola' crossing the lake.

edge in both directions along the lake. Coniston Water is 5¼ miles long, making it the third longest of the sixteen lakes in the Lake District,. Even so, that is only half as long as Windermere, which is the longest lake in England.

11. **At the end of the field climb the stile and cross the footbridge over the stream. Continue ahead along the gravel path above the shingle beach.**

☺ There is another campsite now on the right. Along this part of the path there are many plants with prickles: hawthorn, gorse and thistles, and also nettles, which do not have prickles, but they can of course sting you if you touch them.

See if you can spot the lifebelt on the shingle beach. It is a red and white ring which will float if it is thrown into the water. If someone cannot swim the lifebelt will help keep them afloat. Water can be dangerous, so if you can't already swim, it might be a good idea to learn.

Q: What sort of boats cannot be launched from this beach? Look for a metal sign which will tell you the answer.

A: Motor boats cannot be launched from here, only rowing or sailing boats.

☺ Further along the beach there are probably boats pulled up on the shingle, mainly canoes and rowing boats.

12. **Keep straight ahead and avoid the trackway leading off to the right, away from the lake. The path climbs slightly above the beach. Cross the stile and continue ahead, passing behind the boats and boat-house.**

☺ Down on the left there is a stone boat-house, where boats can be kept. Also there is a wooden pier or 'jetty' where boats can be launched onto the lake.

13. **Go through the gate, onto Torver Commons. Either continue along the trackway through the woods, or bear left through the trees and walk along the beach.**

☺ The woods are made up mainly of oak trees, so keep a look out on the ground for acorns, and also watch out for squirrels, who like to eat acorns. Several small streams run through the woods and lead to the lake. At the other end of the lake a river carries the water on to the sea.

14. **After a short way the Coniston launch jetty should come into view and the boat will return you to the starting point.**

Coniston Water Checklist

- ☐ A seagull
- ☐ A swan
- ☐ A black cow
- ☐ A brown cow
- ☐ A white house
- ☐ A green tent
- ☐ A sheep
- ☐ A peacock
- ☐ A caravan
- ☐ A motor boat
- ☐ A boat with a sail
- ☐ A boat with oars

3. Cunswick Scar

Another area less frequented by the tourist, up in the hills above the town of Kendal, right on the eastern edge of the Lake District, and well worth a visit.

Starting Point: The car park (SD489924) next to the transmitter, on Underbarrow Road, west of Kendal. There is also another car park a short way further along the road.

By Rail: Nearest station: Kendal, 2 miles from starting point

Distance: Entire route: 6 miles. Shorter route (via escape route): just under 3 miles

Terrain: Public paths and bridleways across grassy fields and stony trackways & farm driveways. Some uphill stretches.

Maps: OS outdoor leisure 7, OS Landranger 97

Public Toilets: Nearest toilets: Kendal

Refreshments: Plenty of choice in Kendal

1. **From the first car park, follow the stony trackway through the trees towards the transmitter, signed 'permitted path to Cunswick Fell'. Over on the right there should be a drystone wall.**

☺ You may have noticed that the ground at the car park was white stone. This is called 'limestone' and it has been quarried in this area for hundreds of years. If you look at the wall through the trees (on your right) you will see that this is made of limestone.

Limestone is still quarried in the area today. It is used as stone for building, it is used to make cement and gardeners use it, because it is good for the soil.

2. **Pass the transmitter on the left and follow the stony path through the trees, keeping right to a gate in the drystone wall.**

☺ There are many wild plants and flowers growing in the woods, including blackberries, dandelions, nettles and yellow poppies.

3. **Go through the gate and continue ahead along the edge of the field,**

Looking towards Cunswick Scar (tree-covered, on the right)

**keeping the wall on your left. It is a well worn path and doesn't
run rigidly along the wall, but it should be in sight on your left at
all times.**

☺ There are often cows or sheep in this field. Look out after a short
way for a 'sheep hole' in the wall: a gateway that the sheep can
walk through to get from this field to the next one. Look out for
clumps of wool on the ground.

You can see outcrops of limestone in several places in the field.
Over on the far right you might be able to see where limestone is
still quarried today.
In the field there are several gorse bushes, which are dark and
very prickly. They have yellow flowers in the summer. Gorse
bushes make a good place for rabbits and hares to shelter where
they cannot be seen or disturbed. Another prickly bush there are
a lot of in this area are hawthorns, which have white or pink
blossoms in the spring, and red berries in the autumn.

4. **You should soon come to a crossroads of footpaths, where there
    is a signpost. Continue ahead to the end of the wall, signed again
    for Cunswick Fell. At the corner of the wall follow the sign**

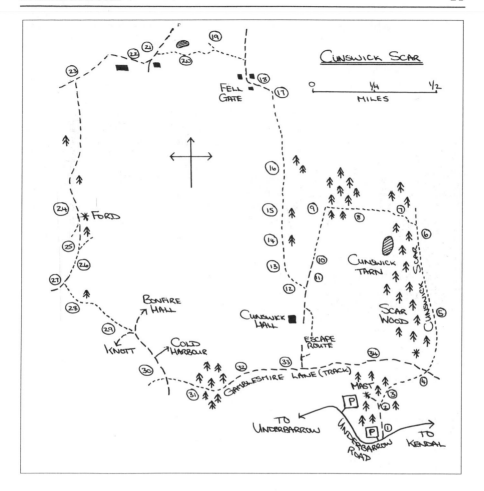

diagonally left. (Again, the path does not run in the shadow of the wall, but it should be kept in sight.)

☺ In the summer there are many flowers growing in the grass, including red clover, daisies and dandelions. See if you can find a dandelion leaf. They have jagged edges, which look like teeth, and in fact the plant gets its name from the French for 'lion's tooth': 'dent de lion'.

5.   **Climb the stile over the fence and continue ahead, with the wall still on your left.**

☺ After a while the wall is replaced by a fence, and there are views on the left over the trees to grassy fields, where there will probably be cows and sheep. In the distance, unless it is misty, you should be able to see the high, rocky fells in the middle of the Lake District, including the well known Langdale Pikes.

6. **Keep a look out for the gate in the fence on the left. Go through and bear slightly to the left, around the bushes, then follow the winding rocky path downhill through the trees.**

☺ The rocky path leads downhill through the shady woods. It is quite damp, and there is moss on many of the rocks and tree trunks. Look out for fungus growing on fallen logs, and also keep an eye open for squirrels in the branches overhead. Most importantly take care on the way downhill, as it is easy to stumble or slip!

7. **Keep to the main path, which is rocky in places. At the bottom of the woods bear right across the stile and follow the path straight ahead to the kissing gate. Go through and follow the direction sign across the open field, towards the edge of the woods opposite.**

☺ There should be a small pond, or 'tarn' over on your left, and in the distance you should be able to see the transmitter near the car park. That should give you some idea of how far you've walked. You should be able to see it from various points along the walk.

8. **Go through the gap in the drystone wall in the far right corner of the field. Follow the path straight ahead through the woods.**

☺ There are many small plants growing on the ground in these woods. This is known as 'undergrowth' because it grows under the trees. You might be able to smell an onion-like smell. This is from a plant called 'wood garlic' which has white flowers in the spring and summer, and can often be found growing in damp, shady woods.

There are several different types of trees here, including sycamore and beech, which are popular with squirrels, because they have nuts on in the autumn, which the squirrels can eat. Also, if you are quiet you might be lucky enough to see red deer grazing amongst the trees, but they are nervous creatures and will run away at the slightest sound.

9. **At the other end of the woods go through the gap in the wall and bear left along the edge of the field.**

☺ There are open fields to the right, where there might be cows. Look out for thistles in the grass, which have prickly leaves and grow quite tall. In the summer they have tufty purple flowers. After a short way you should be able to see a white stone farmhouse ahead.

10. **Keep along the wall, straight ahead. The path soon becomes a trackway, leading towards the farm.**

    The farmers may use electric fences in this area. They should all be labelled as such, and are not dangerous, but will give a mild shock if you grab hold of them, so be warned.

11. **Go through a sprung wooden gate and continue towards the farmhouse for a short way, until the track joins the farm driveway. At this point go through a further wooden gate off to the right and continue across the grassy field towards the stile, clearly visible ahead.**

    Escape route/shorter route: Continue ahead along the driveway towards the farm. After a short way take the wooden gate on the left just before the farmhouse, and bear right towards a further gate. Continue ahead along the edge of the field. Towards the end of the field there is a gate on the right. Go through and bear left to the top of the field. Continue from direction 33.

12. **Climb the stile and bear diagonally right, passing the farmhouse on the left.**

Q: In this field there may be thistles, buttercups and hawthorns. Which one of these does NOT have prickles?

A: Buttercups, which are the yellow flowers amongst the grass. Look out also for nettles, which can sting you if you touch them.

13. **Towards the bottom of the field there are directional arrows, pointing along a rough grassy trackway, leading off to the right between hawthorn bushes. (Heading in a roughly northerly direction).**

☺ Prickly hawthorn bushes like these are popular places for certain birds, like black and white magpies, to build their nests, because they will be protected by all the sharp thorns. Can you see any nests between the branches?

14. At the end of the track continue ahead across the small field and climb the stile. Continue ahead through the next field, with the hedge on your left.

15. After a short way look out for a gap in the dry stone wall on the left. Go through this and bear right along the edge of the field. Go through the metal gate, but take care, as there may be further electric fences in operation. Bear diagonally left across the field.

☺ There are mixed hedges along the edges of these fields, made up of many different plants and bushes, including holly, hawthorn, nettles, and purple bell-shaped flowers called foxgloves. There may be cows or sheep grazing in the fields.

16. Go through the gateway in the left corner of the field. Avoid the gate on the left and keep straight ahead, going through the wooden five bar gate opposite. Keep straight ahead across the field. There is no clear path at first, but head towards the white cottage in the distance.

☺ Again there may be cows or sheep in this field, but look out also for wild animals running for the cover of the hedges, such as rabbits, hares or foxes. Hares are very similar to rabbits, except they are larger and have longer ears. Their back legs are very powerful, and they can run over 30 miles an hour, which is faster than a car should travel on most roads in the town. Foxes are related to dogs. They have a reddish coat on top and are usually white underneath. They are famous for their thick, bushy tails.

17. The path leads slightly downhill. Towards the bottom of the field it becomes easier to follow, turning into a clear rutted trackway, bearing round to the left, through a gateway in a hawthorn hedge.

18. Follow the trackway as it winds towards the farm buildings. Pass the farmhouse on your right. Keep right after the farmhouse and go through the gateway. Bear left after a short way, along a stony trackway, leading slightly uphill.

Q: How many chimneys does the farmhouse have?

A: Two.

19. **Go through the gateway barring the trackway. Soon after this the track splits in two. Keep left along the undulating track, with the wall close on your left.**

☺ In the distance on the left you should be able to see the transmitter again, rising up above the treetops. This is about the half way point of the walk.

20. **Keep ahead along the wall, avoiding the ladder stile to the left. After a short way some rooftops should come into view ahead.**

☺ Over on the right there is a small tarn, with many grass-like reeds around it. A lot of new trees have been planted in this area, and might still be in plastic tubing, to protect them from animals who might eat their soft, young bark.

21. **After the tarn the path bears away from the wall, and leads uphill towards the rooftops. Go through the five bar gate onto the farm driveway. Bear left.**

☺ This is a very old road, called Capplerigg Lane. It is named after the rocky fell over on the right, called Capple Rigg. 'Rigg' is a local word for 'ridge', which is like a platform.

There may be hens running freely around the garden of the house on the left.

22. **Bear right along the well signed public bridleway to Lindreth Brow. Go through the metal gate and follow the stony trackway.**

Q: There are occasional trees along the trackway, including oak and holly. One of these trees is an 'evergreen', which means it doesn't lose its leaves in the winter, but which one?

A: Holly is an evergreen, which is why it is often used as part of Christmas decorations.

☺ Ivy is another evergreen plant. You may have heard the Christmas carol, 'The Holly and the Ivy'. It can be found growing in places along the wall, climbing over the stones with its tiny suckers.

23. **At the fork bear left, signed as a public bridleway. Keep to the clear trackway ahead at all times. Avoid all gates on both sides.**

☺ There are many plants growing alongside the trackway, and in places there are trees overhanging, making the track shady. On the left you will occasionally have views across the fields that you walked through earlier on in the walk. Can you recognise the route you took?

24. **After some way a stream crosses the path. Cross the small stone footbridge on the left and continue ahead along the trackway.**

☺ **(AT THE STREAM)** This is a 'ford', which is a place where a road passes through a stream or river. The water is quite shallow, so horses, carts and tractors could easily cross.

25. **Soon after the ford go through the five bar gate which bars the trackway and follow the clear track as it leads slightly uphill. There should be an area of woodland over on your left. Keep straight ahead.**

26. **When the path splits, bear right. (There is an old sign pointing the way, signed as a footpath to Underbarrow). The track leads slightly downhill, and there should now be a drystone wall on your right. Go through the five bar gate and continue ahead.**

☺ The trackway might be muddy in places, so look out for the prints made by cows or horses, and see if you can find a footprint smaller than your own.

27. **After a very short way you should come to a junction. Do not carry on ahead through the five bar gate, instead bear left along a pathway leading uphill between hedgerows.**

☺ After a short way you should be able to see the transmitter again, straight ahead.

At the sides of the path there are many plants growing wild, including brambles, nettles, dock, hawthorn, holly, bracken, ivy, buttercups, foxgloves, young oaks, dandelions and purple clover. How many can you recognise?

Q: Two of these plants have yellow flowers. Which ones?

A: Buttercups and dandelions.

28. **The path undulates fairly frequently. It eventually leads down to a tarmac farm driveway. Continue straight ahead, leading uphill, passing on the right a gateway and cattle grid leading to 'Knott'.**

☺ Look out for wild raspberries in the hedgerows. They have prickly stems, like blackberries, and grow upright and have red fruit in the late summer and autumn. See if you can see any rabbit holes leading into the grassy banks along the lane.

Q: After a short way you should pass a farmhouse on the left. How many chimneys does it have?

A. Two. One on either side of the main roof.

29. Continue ahead, crossing the cattle grid (there is a gate to the right for dogs). Follow the main driveway.

Q: What is the name of the farm on the left?

A. You should find the name painted on a slate at the gateway to the farm. It's called "Cold Harbour".

☺ A little way further on you will come to an open grassy area where there may be cows grazing. In bad weather hay may be put out for them to eat. There are also quite often hens running around free here.

30. Avoid the public footpath off to the right. Instead take the gate on the left signed as a public bridleway.

(Note: there are various gates off to the left, make sure it is the signed bridleway which you take.

31. After a short way the path leads into an area of woodland. Keep straight ahead along the main path.

☺ The path leads slightly uphill through the shady woods. Some of the trees have been cut down and you might be able to see the stumps that are left. Others have fallen over and you should be able to see their roots sticking up in the air. The woods are quite wet and shaded from the sun by all the trees, many of which have moss growing on their bark. Look out for rabbits on the ground, or squirrels in the treetops.

32. At the end of the woods go through the five bar wooden gate and continue ahead along the trackway.

☺ Over on the left is a farm (Cunswick Hall) and again there are good views over the countryside you have walked through.

33. Go through the metal gate and continue along the trackway. There

are various gates barring the trackway. Go through these, keeping
with the main trackway at all times as it winds uphill.

☺ Up on right above trees you should be able to see the transmitter.
Not far to go now......

As you get nearer to the top of the trackway, you should be able
to see on the left what looks like the arch of a tunnel built into the
hillside. It is actually a 'lime kiln', which is a type of 'furnace' or
oven for heating pieces of locally quarried limestone to extract
the lime.

34. **The path leads back to the crossroads of footpaths, which you
should recognise from earlier on. Bear right, signed for Scout Scar,
returning along the edge of the field towards the transmitter. Go
through the gate in the woods and bear left. Keep left, back to the
car park.**

Cunswick Scar Checklist

☐ A yellow flower

☐ A blue flower

☐ A horse

☐ A black and white cow

☐ A brown cow

☐ A squirrel

☐ A sheep with a white face

☐ A sheep with a black face

☐ A stone bridge

☐ A bird's feather

☐ A fircone

☐ A hen or cockerel

☐ A white house

☐ A deer

4. Easedale

Grasmere is the heart of Wordsworth country, and Easedale was one of his favourite walking areas, particularly to and around Easedale Tarn. This route is popular at the weekend, and understandably so. The climb up to the tarn is, on the whole, gradual, and the relatively short distance gives a real sense of achievement. Those without stout, waterproof footwear should return the same way to avoid the potentially soggy areas on the homeward journey.

Starting Point: The village green (owned by the National Trust) in the centre of Grasmere Village (NY337076). To make the route shorter start from the Easedale road car park (NY334080). Bear right along the lane and begin with direction 2

By Bus: Services right to the village green from Kendal, Windermere, Ambleside, Keswick and Carlisle

Distance: Entire circular route: 4½ miles

Terrain: Rocky pathways; a steady ascent towards the tarn. Possibly some water-logged areas on return section

Maps: OS Landranger 90, OS Outdoor Leisure 7

Public Toilets: Behind the village green

Refreshments: The Lancrigg Country House Hotel serves tea and snacks to walkers. Leave your boots in the porch! There are various places in Grasmere village, though the Rowan Tree overlooking the river and church is particularly recommended for a sunny day

☺ **(AT THE GREEN)** Can you see the bus shelter? There is a plaque on it's wall celebrating the "Silver Jubilee" of Queen Elizabeth II, which was when she had been queen for 25 years.

Q: In which year was that?

A: The Queen's Silver Jubilee, as it says on the plaque, was in 1977, probably a long time before you were born.

1. **From the village green take Easedale Road, leading away opposite, to the right of the Heaton Cooper Studios, signed for "Easedale Tarn".**

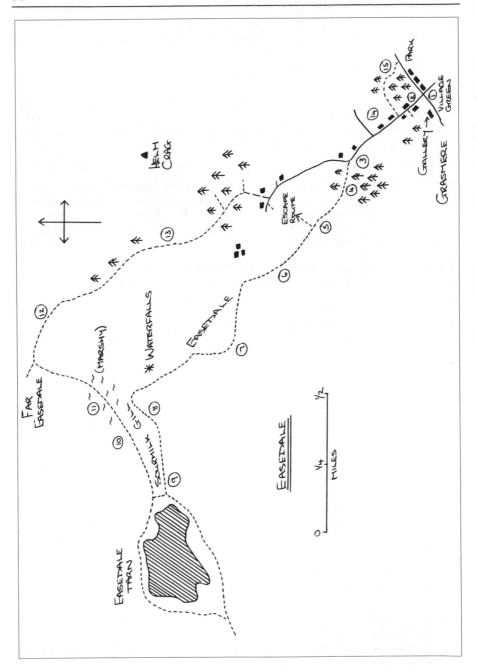

EASEDALE

☺ This is Grasmere, famous for once being the home of the poet, William Wordsworth, who lived here 200 years ago. For eight years he lived in a small cottage on the other side of the village, (Now called "Dove Cottage" and open to the public) where he wrote some of his best-loved poems.

This lane leads away from the village between "drystone" walls with many mosses and ferns growing on them. They are called "drystone" because, as you can see, there is no cement to hold the stones together. All over the Lake District there are walls like this, even very high up on the fells, and many of them were built hundreds of years ago, but were so well put together that they have lasted well and have needed little or no repairs.

When you are walking along a road you should always keep well in to the side and should always walk TOWARDS the traffic. For example, keep your RIGHT hand close to the wall, hedge or fence, so that you are always aware of the traffic as it comes towards you.

Q: What is the name of the first house on the right?

A: Dockwray Cottage

Shortly on the left there should be views over to a large house called 'Allan Bank', where the Wordsworths lived, very unhappily, for a short time. In the end they were forced to leave because the chimneys smoked so badly. Dorothy wrote how she had to dust continually to remove the thick black grime from the furniture.

☺ Further on, also on the right, look out for a 'weather-vane' on a roof in the shape of a cockerel. Weather-vanes show which direction the wind is blowing. Can you tell which way it is blowing today?

2. **In a short way there is a permitted footpath on the left, which will keep you off the road for some way. At the end continue along the lane.**

☺ The road soon crosses Easedale Beck, which flows very fast after heavy rain. The bridge, by the way, is called 'Goody Bridge'.

Q: In a short way you should be able to see a round road-sign with a car and motorbike on it. What do you think this means? (This is quite a hard one, I think, so here's a clue: circular roadsigns with red borders are usually telling you not to do something.)

A: The sign means that no motor vehicles are allowed past this point, except for people who happen to live further along the lane, so still be on the look-out for oncoming cars.

Q: Look out for the name-plate of a farmhouse with yellow flowers on it. What is the name of the farm, and what are the flowers called?

A: The farm is called 'Goody Bridge Farm', after the bridge you just crossed over, and the flowers are, of course, daffodils, which are very common here in the spring.

☺ Further on again on the right, keep a look out for a post-box built into the wall, with the initials E II R on it, which stand for Elizabeth II, the present queen.

3. **The road soon bears to the right. At this point cross the footbridge on the left and continue straight ahead through the trees. Cross the stone slab bridge and continue ahead along a stony, partially cobbled pathway.**

☺ The stream is the same one you crossed earlier, Easedale Beck. It gets its name from the valley of Easedale, which you are about to enter. The beck carries all the water that runs down from the high fells that surround this area. The path is a bridleway, which means horses can also use it.

4. **Go through the iron gate and continue along the path. The stream should now be on your right.**

☺ Straight ahead, in Easedale, you should be able to see a stream tumbling down over rocks. This is called Sour Milk Gill, and after heavy rain it is a very impressive sight and can be heard from some distance away.

On the right, the rocky fell is known as 'the Lion and the Lamb' because some of the rocks at the top seem to be in the shape of these two animals, though they are not visible from this angle.

5. **The path soon draws near to the stream. Do not cross the bridge. Continue ahead.**

(Escape route: Cross the bridge and follow the footpath over the fields. Go through the gate and follow the trackway to the lane. Bear right for Grasmere village)

Looking down on Easedale Tarn

☺ If you look back over your shoulder you should now be able to see some of the high fells which surround the village of Grasmere. You might be able to make out the lines of the drystone walls which stretch right up towards the tops. The fells are green in the spring and summer, but in the autumn the bracken, which covers most of their slopes, dies and turns a gold or rusty brown colour.

The stream alongside the path has very clear water and you should be able to see the stones along the bottom. There are several trees and bushes overhanging the water, including blackberries with their long prickly stems and dog roses, which have pink flowers in spring and bright red rosehips in the autumn.

6. **Avoid the gate off to the left, signed as a public footpath. Continue ahead, signed for Easedale Tarn. After some way go through a metal gate barring the trackway, cross the stream and continue ahead along the main path, signed as a public bridleway. Note: the main path at this point veers slightly away from the stream and heads uphill towards the falls. Do not take the path to the right which continues for a short way along the stream.**

☺ By now you should certainly be able to hear the roaring of the falls. This was one of the favourite places of the poet, Wordsworth, who liked to come walking here with his sister. He loved all the Lake District and wrote most of his poems about the places he had visited, but this valley was one of the places he loved the most.

There should soon be views into the valley, over marshy fields surrounded by yet more drystone walls. In the fields there are often cows and sheep, and perhaps wild rabbits nibbling at the grass.

7.   Go through the various gates barring the trackway and continue uphill, but do not stray from the main path and avoid all gateways.

☺ From here on there are occasional 'grooves' made in the path. These are drainage channels, which allow rainwater to drain properly, so that the paths will not get waterlogged. There are many small mountain streams crossing the path which are called 'tributaries' and run into the main beck in the bottom of the valley. In turn, the beck runs into a river, which will eventually take all the water to the sea.

Also in places the path has been cobbled by the National Trust, who own the valley, so that the path does not wear away with the hundreds of feet that pass along here every week. The Lake District is a very popular place for walking, and if the paths are not looked after properly they can soon get damaged.

(There is a grassy trackway off to the right, leading downhill between drystone walls . This gives access to the bottom of the falls, but return the same way to the main path and continue ahead.)

☺ On the left of the path there are rocks showing from beneath the soil, which have water running over them almost all the time. This makes them an ideal home for moisture-loving ferns and mosses which cling to the surface of the stone.

As the path gets higher you should be able to look back along the valley and see the rooftops of the village of Grasmere, where the walk began. Notice how there are fewer trees now you are higher up. There are more rocks and boulders lying about, more bracken, and occasionally a straggly hawthorn bush. There may also be sheep roaming freely here, chewing away amongst the bracken, so don't be startled if one suddenly darts out in front of you.

(There is easy access to the falls ahead, where there is a large pool for paddling)

☺ The stream looks very inviting in warm weather, but never play in or near water without an adult's permission. If you are allowed to paddle take care. Wet rocks can be slippery!

8. **Continue ahead after the falls. The path gets flatter for a short way and passes an area of marsh alongside the stream, after which there is the final winding climb up to the tarn.**

☺ Higher still, and there are even fewer trees now. It seems more open and lonelier, as there is no sign of the village or any houses at all, only the grassy slopes of the high fells.

And eventually...... at the top of the path is Easedale Tarn. ('Tarn' is a local word meaning pond or pool.) In the summer there are lilies floating on the surface of the water and reads around the edges. This was the favourite tarn of the poet, Wordsworth, and he often walked here from his home in Grasmere.
At one time there was a stone hut selling refreshments here to the *many* walkers that passed by on their way to the high fells that surround you. It is no longer here, but if you look carefully you might be able to see its ruins on the opposite side of the tarn.

(To avoid possible water-logged areas return the same way to Grasmere)

9. **Either walk all the way around the tarn, keeping close to the water's edge, or bear right and cross the stepping stones at the head of the stream. Bear right along the rocky path, which winds between bracken and boulders and leads downhill. The stream should be fairly close on the right for some way.**

☺ It can be very marshy here, so I hope you've got your wellies on! Ahead is another view of the Lion and the Lamb.

10. **The path can get hard to follow here, so be vigilant. It soon bears to the left, away from the stream. On your right now there should be an area of marsh, and on your left are bracken covered slopes. Follow the stepping stones over the most boggy areas. (If you're careful it is usually possible to get the whole way without getting your feet wet.)**

11. **The path skirts the marsh and returns fairly close to the stream. The path now leads to the left, away from the stream, and through bracken, beginning to lead downhill. At this point you should be**

able to see down into the next valley. There are occasional
National Trust signs pointing the way to Grasmere, and various
yellow arrows though the path soon becomes wide and easy to
follow.

☺ The sound of the beck suddenly stops, but as you descend there
is the sound of rushing water from another stream in a different
valley, called Far Easedale.

12. **Bear left as you approach the drystone wall. Soon the path bears
right, downhill, close to the wall. At the bottom bear right to the
stream and cross the wooden bridge. Bear right along the stream,
keeping close to its bank for some way. From now on the path is
easy to follow.**

☺ The bridge over the stream wobbles slightly as you cross, but
don't worry, it's quite safe. There are several colourful rowan
trees along the stream. In the spring they are covered with
blossom, and in the autumn they have clusters of bright red
berries, which are eaten by many small birds and animals. Again
there are several 'tributaries' crossing the path and also drainage
ditches.

There are many nice places to stop and rest or picnic along the
stream, which is called Far Easedale Gill. This joins Easedale
Beck which you walked along earlier. As you might guess, 'Gill'
and 'Beck' are both local words meaning stream.

13. **Soon the stream veers away and passes out of sight. Continue
ahead and keep to the main stony path. Shortly there is a craggy
descent, and often small streams running along the path. Take
care on the rocks.**

☺ There should now be drystone walls on both sides of the path,
and look out for the stone barn on the left. After a short way the
waterfall should come into sight again, over on the right.

Notice how there are more trees now that you have come down
from the higher ground. Trees need a lot of water, so they tend
to grow along the streams and in the lower land.

14. **Pass the farm on the right and continue ahead along the main
pathway. There is an area of woodland on the left and later on
both sides.**

☺ If you're tall enough to see over the walls, you should be able to
see how the middle of the valley is wide and flat now, and there

are probably sheep grazing in the fields. You might also be able to see people walking along the path towards the tarn.

The woods along the path are mainly beech and oak trees. Both these trees have 'fruit' in the autumn: beech-nuts and acorns. See if you can see any on the ground. They provide food for hungry squirrels in the cold winter months. There are also holly bushes in the woods. The fruit of the holly bush is its red berries. All trees and plants have 'fruit', but that doesn't mean it is alright to eat, because many wild berries and nuts are poisonous to humans, even though animals can eat them.

15. At the junction keep right, signed for 'Grasmere'. Go through the long gate and follow the slate path downhill between cottages.

Q: At the bottom of the slate path there is a gate with the name of a cottage on it. What is it called?

A: 'Jackdaw Cottage'. A jackdaw is a bird, similar to a crow. There is also a gate leading to 'Easedale House'.

16. Bear left at the bottom and follow the main tarmac drive, passing further cottages, then grass on either side. Keep straight ahead.

(From the driveway across the field you can see a large rock in the field on the left, which was mentioned frequently by Dorothy Wordsworth in her Grasmere journals. She came here often on cold winters days and "walked up and down". The large house in the background was owned by friends of the Wordsworths. It is now 'Lancrigg Vegetarian Hotel', which serves afternoon tea and snacks to walkers.)

☺ Look back now, and you should have a good view of the Sour Milk Gill waterfalls, and you can see how far you've walked.

17. Continue ahead. Go the open gateway and follow the lane, passing the footbridge on the right.

☺ Soon you will be able to see the stream on your right. Can you see where a trackway once ran through a shallow part of the water? This is called a 'ford' and it was the only way across for vehicles and carts heading into Easedale.

Q: What is the name of the house opposite the ford?

A: Oak Lodge

18. Continue ahead along the lane.

Q: Look out for a round roadsign with '30' on it. What do you think
    this means?

A: It means that the maximum speed is 30 miles an hour.

19. **Follow the lane and permitted footpath. After some way look out
    for the guesthouse on the left called 'Silverlea.' Directly after it go
    through the gate and along the footpath through the woods,
    Butterlyp How.**

    Escape route: Continue ahead along the lane into Grasmere village.

☺ These woods contain many mixed trees. See if you can recognise
    any of them. This was yet another favourite place of the poet,
    Wordsworth, where he and his sister could come for a short walk
    if the weather was not good enough for them to travel further.

    Soon you might be able to hear the sound of the river, which
    should come into view below on your left, through the leaves of
    the trees. From here it runs through the village and empties into
    Grasmere lake. At the other end of the lake it continues on
    through two more lakes before it reaches the sea.

20. **At the end of the woods go through the gate and bear right along
    the lane, passing the park on the left. Continue ahead back to the
    village.**

    (In the park there is a children's adventure playground).

Easedale Checklist

☐ A post box

☐ A stone bridge

☐ A daffodil

☐ A horse

☐ Someone with a dog

☐ A metal gate

☐ A sheep

☐ A chimney pot

☐ A tree with red berries

☐ A tree with prickles

5. Elterwater & the Forces and Little Langdale

Some of the most attractive countryside in Lakeland, and two waterfalls, one (Skelwith Force) having the distinction of carrying a greater volume of water than any other force in the Lake District. There's even an optional pub detour in Little Langdale.

There is an unavoidable short stretch along the main road at Skelwith Bridge, that being the only river crossing for miles. (It's a great shame that the National Trust haven't built a footbridge to link their properties on either side of the river, but unfortunately they haven't.) To avoid this, stick to the shorter route, following the last escape route back to Elterwater.

Starting Point: Outside the Britannia Inn, in the centre of the village. (NY328048). From the Skelwith Bridge to Great Langdale road the village is signed off to the left, 'Elterwater ¼ mile. Follow the road into the village centre, where the pub is on the right with the toilets on the left. There are various car parks between the B road and the village, and also a National Trust car park through the village and on the left before the river.

By Bus: The 'Langdale Rambler' service, from Ambleside – stops at the Britannia Inn.

Distance: Entire route: 6 miles. Via escape route: 4 miles

Terrain: Stony trackways, farm driveways, some uphill stretches. As mentioned above there is a short stretch along the main road at Skelwith Bridge which can be avoided by using the escape route.

Maps: OS Outdoor Leisure 7, OS Landranger 90

Public Toilets: Elterwater village

Refreshments: Elterwater village: pub. Skelwith Bridge: cafés, pub

---

☺ **(OUTSIDE THE INN)** The village is named after the nearby lake of Elterwater. As you can see by looking around, most of the houses are built of a grey stone called 'slate', which is quarried very near to here. In fact, you may hear the sounds of the quarry. Stone is blasted from a 'cliff face' using explosives, so you may hear the bang and feel the rumblings in the ground, so don't be

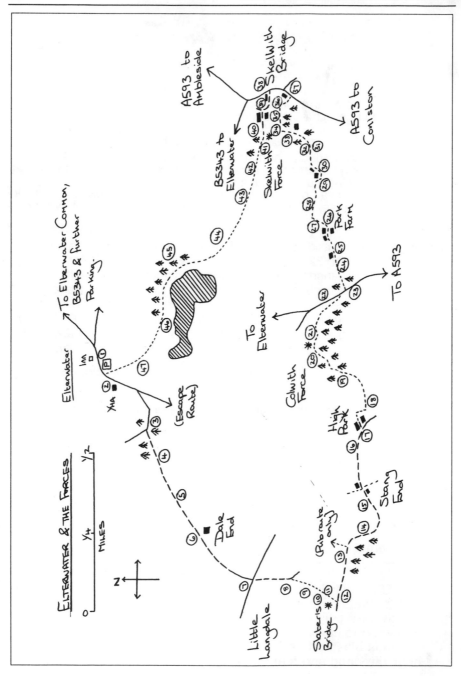

startled. There should be a siren sounded before any blasting takes place, so if you hear it you can get ready for the bang. If you have a dog which is easily frightened it might be a good idea to put it on its lead.

The pub, the Britannia Inn, is in the middle of the village. It was built as a farmhouse in the 17th Century, nearly 400 years ago. (There are seats outside overlooking the village green.)

1. **From the inn follow the main village road downhill towards the stream, passing the toilets on your left, then the National Trust car park. Cross over the bridge and follow the road around to the left.**

☺ This bridge was built 300 years ago and crosses Great Langdale Beck. If you look over you will see the water is very clear, and there are stones on the bottom, many of which are slate.

Q: There is a slate plaque on the bridge. What does it say?

A: It says Elterwater Bridge.

2. **Pass the youth hostel on the right, soon after which bear right, along the narrow lane leading uphill.**

☺ On the left you should pass a barn which has been converted into a holiday home. This is quite common these days as the Lake District is so popular with walkers and tourists.

The tourist industry is now the principle employer & earner in the Lake District.

☺ Next on the left you should pass the stone gateway to Elterwater Hall. In the gardens of the hall there are many rhododendron bushes, which have many large, colourful flowers in the summer. Here the lane is shaded with overhanging trees.

3. **As the road bears around to the right, keep left along the narrow lane leading uphill, signed as a footpath to Little Langdale. Also signed as unsuitable for motors, and soon degenerating into a stony trackway. Avoid all paths, gates and stiles to either side, and keep straight ahead along the main track.**

Q: As you leave the road there is a sign with a 'T' on it. What do you think this means?

Looking over Elterwater and surrounding countryside

A: It means the road ahead is a dead end, and there is no way through for cars.

😊 The trackway is covered with loose slate. As well as the working quarry at Elterwater, there are several other quarries in this area which are now closed. There are many wild plants along the side of the trackway, including nettles, holly and blackberries. On the drystone walls there is moss growing, and small, moisture-loving ferns, and ivy clings to the stone with its tiny suckers.

In the woods on the right of the track there are many tall, old trees, and a lot of birds. After some way the woods finish and there are grassy fields with buttercups. At this point look back for views over the countryside below. As you continue further along the track you should be able to look back and see Elterwater in the distance, surrounded by trees and reeds.

4.   **Go through the five bar gate and continue ahead. The track is flatter from now on. Again avoid all paths, stiles and gates to either side and keep to the main track.**

😊 Up on the right are the grassy slopes of Lingmoor Fell, which has many disused quarries around it. There are better views around to Lingmoor as the path bends. You may be able to see stony crags and some of the slate left over from the quarrying. 'Ling' means heather, and the fell gets its name because the top is almost entirely covered with heather.

There may be sheep along the trackway, or in the fields on either side. Some of the fields are used to make hay. This is grass which is allowed to grow tall, then in the late summer it is cut and left to dry before being taken into barns where it can be used for winter food for cows and horses. Sometimes the hay is wrapped in black plastic and left in the fields, looking like large dustbin bags.

5. **Go through a further gate barring the track and continue ahead.**

Q: You should by now be able to see rooftops in front of you, which is part of a farmhouse you will soon pass. How many chimneys are there on the farmhouse?

A: Three. Two on the main roof and one on a lower roof.

6. **Pass the farmhouse and farm buildings (Dale End) on the left and continue ahead. The track bears round to the right and becomes a tarmac road leading gradually downhill.**

☺ There are occasional views to the left between the bushes and trees over the valley of Little Langdale. You might be able to see stone cottages or white farmhouses and in winter there will be smoke rising from the chimneys. Towards the bottom of the driveway, Little Langdale Tarn comes into view.

7. **At the lane bear left for a very short way, then take the driveway to Birk Howe Farm, off to the right.**

☺ Downhill on the right is the tarn, which is private, so you cannot go any nearer than this. It is marshy around the edges of the water, and there are grass-like reeds growing. In bad weather there are often seagulls around the tarn, and it is the home of many rare geese and other water birds.

8. **After a short way the drive bears around to the left to the farm- house. At this point bear right through a five bar gate. There is a slate sign on the wall pointing the way: 'To Slater's Bridge, keep dogs on leads'. Follow the stony trackway downhill. Go through**

a further gate and keep straight ahead with a drystone wall on your left.

☺ On the hillside ahead there are piles of loose slate left over from more quarrying.

9. **Go through the kissing gate and keep straight ahead as the path winds downhill.**

☺ This stream leaves the tarn and carries on through Little Langdale. It has many reeds along its banks, and in the summer there are water-lilies floating on its surface. Several streams enter the tarn at the other end, bringing water down from the high fells in the distance.

10. **Avoid the path off to the left. Keep straight ahead to the bridge.**

☺ This is Slater's Bridge. As you can see, it is made of stone and is very old. It was once used by the quarry men (or 'slaters') to carry slabs of slate across the stream from the quarry. If you look over into the water, you should see that the rocks and pebbles on the bottom are covered with a hair-like weed which sways in the water.

11. **After the bridge go up the steps and through the gap in the drystone wall. Follow the clear stony pathway straight ahead. Go through the gate and bear left along the trackway . Keep to the main path.**

12. **Keep to the lower path, with the stream a short way over on your left. Go through the various gates barring the trackway, but do not go through any gate leading off to the right, which will take you onto the quarry scars.**

☺ On the left is a small grassy field, where there might be sheep. Beyond that is the stream. Along the trackway there are trees and bushes, including hawthorn and holly, which both have red berries in the autumn, which are eaten by birds and other small animals through the winter months when there is little else to eat. Even in the snow the bright red berries can be spotted by the eyes of hungry creatures. You, however, should never eat wild berries. Just because animals eat them it doesn't mean they are safe for humans to eat.

The path soon drops down into an area of oak woodland, so look out for acorns on the ground.

Pub route: Cross the bridge and follow the lane uphill. Bear right at the top. The Three Shires Inn is a short way on the left. Return the same way to continue with the route.

☺ Just past the wooden bridge is a 'ford', which is a place where a road or trackway goes through a stream or river. You can see there aren't any big stones in the water, and it is very shallow, so carts and horses could easily cross over.

13. **Do not cross the bridge. Continue past it and then follow the main path uphill, leading away from the stream. Avoid minor paths off to either side. At the fork, keep left, signed for Colwith & Skelwith.**

☺ The path leads between oak trees and also silver birches, which have thin trunks with whitish bark. After a short way the path crosses a stream by an arched stone bridge. Notice along the banks of the stream there are ferns and mosses growing, and a white-flowering plant called 'wood garlic' which can often be found in damp places. It has a strong garlic or onion smell.

14. **The track soon becomes a well maintained tarmac driveway, curving slightly uphill to the left. Keep to the main drive.**

15. **Follow the driveway as it winds uphill, over a cattlegrid (or through the gate next to it). Avoid the signed footpath off to the left. Continue between the farm buildings.**

☺ The white farmhouse is one of the buildings you may have been able to see from across the valley earlier on in the walk. Over on the right is a stone barn with a balcony. This is a 'spinning gallery' and was where the farmer's wife would sit spinning sheep's wool into thick yarn or thread. Today it is often used for storing logs for the fire.

16. **Keep to the main driveway, which winds around the farmhouse and bears off to the left, signed again for Colwith & Skelwith. Avoid all stiles and gateways on either side and keep to the main driveway.**

☺ There are good views on the left, downhill over grassy fields and over the valley. Can you make out where you walked earlier?

17. **After a short way the drive leads round to another farmhouse. Avoid the path off to the left and continue towards the farm. Go through the five bar gate on the left into the farmyard. Bear round**

to the right and look out for the kissing gate on the left. Go through this and follow the clear path ahead.

Q: There are usually hens running free in the corner of this field. Hens are female. Do you know what the male bird is called?

A: A cockerel.

18. Go through a gate and bear left, with the drystone wall on your left. Go through the gate into the National Trust woodland and take the first path off to the left, leading downhill through the trees, signed 'Permissive Path to Colwith Force'.

☺ The path leads downhill through the woods, where there are many different types of trees, plants and flowers. Look out for fir-cones, acorns, squirrels and rabbits, and watch out, because the path might be boggy in places, especially after a lot of rain.

19. Follow the path for some way, still downhill, crossing several streams. Keep to the main path, which is quite easy to follow at this point. Under a large beech tree the path bears to the right.

☺ After a while you should be able to hear the sound of a waterfall ahead, and soon a stream comes into view down below on the left. This is the same stream you crossed over earlier on in the walk. Notice how it has trees overhanging it and many of the stones in the water have moss on them.

20. In places the path is not clearly defined. At points it splits and heads in various directions. There is no one correct path, but make sure that the stream is never far from sight on the left. (In the vicinity of the falls take care of the drop down to the water.)

☺ You should soon come to the waterfall, or 'force' as they are called locally. This is known as Colwith Force. There are several streams of water falling over large rocks into a deep pool. For hundreds of years this has been a well known beauty spot.

21. After the falls, continue along the path above the river. Again, don't go very far away from the water on your left. The path winds above the river now, cobbled in places.

Q: The trees are now all deciduous. What does this mean?

A: It means they lose their leaves in the winter. Most of the trees now are oaks. Many of them have moss and lichen growing on their bark.

22. **The path leads down to a stile. Climb this and bear right along the lane.**

    Escape route/shorter route: Bear left along the road and keep straight ahead, which will take you back to Elterwater village. (1 mile)

23. **After a short way along the lane take the slate steps over the drystone wall on the left, signed as a public footpath to Skelwith Bridge. Follow the clear pathway. At the end of the small field it leads uphill through the woods. Some scrambling may be necessary. Keep to the main path.**

☺ Down below you now is the stream which you have followed all the way from Little Langdale. Soon it bears away and empties into Elterwater.

24. **At the top follow the path to the stile and continue along the stony path across the field, towards the farm buildings. Cross the driveway. (The gates to the house should be on your immediate left.) Opposite, sheltered amongst the trees is a stile leading along a shady pathway between bushes and undergrowth. Follow this to the end and go through the gap in the wall.**

Q: Over on the left is the gateway to a cottage. What is it called?

A: 'Ruthwaite'. The name can be found on a plaque on the gate. 'Thwaite' is a local word meaning 'clearing'. It can be found in many Cumbrian place names, like Graythwaite, Esthwaite and Crosthwaite.

26. **Cross the driveway and continue between the farm buildings, with a yellow arrow to point the way. This is Park Farm.**

Q: In which year was the barn on the right built?

A: 1879. The date is chiselled into a stone plaque on the front of the barn.

☺ Look out for swallows, which are small birds with 'V' shaped tails, which fly very close to the ground. They can often be found around farm buildings and where they build their nests. Swallows migrate in the winter, which means they fly south to other countries where it is warmer. Swallows head for Africa, and return to Britain any time after March, when the weather is (usually) beginning to get warmer. They often return to exactly the same places each year.

27. **Continue straight ahead through the farmyard, passing the farmhouse on your left and a wooden chalet on your right. Go through the wooden five bar gate after the farm and follow the stony track downhill.**

28. **At the fork at the bottom bear right, signed for Skelwith Bridge. Go through the five bar gate after the caravans and continue ahead along the clear trackway.**

☺ Again there are many wild plants growing in the grassy field, including nettles, prickly thistles and foxgloves, which are tall plants with purple, bell-like flowers, which are poisonous. There are often sheep in these fields. See if you can find any strands of sheep wool in the grass.

29. **Keep to the main trackway, signed occasionally with yellow arrows. Do not bear off to the left downhill at any point. After some way you should come to a stone house.**

☺ This house is built of stone, mainly slate, and it has a stream running through its garden. In summer there are a lot of colourful water plants growing in or near the water. The house also has a veranda which sometimes has logs under to keep them dry for the fire.

30. **Go through the metal kissing gate and follow the path around the garden. At the end bear right onto the driveway. Pass the cottages on the left and go through the gate barring the trackway. Continue ahead, leading uphill at first.**

☺ On the left through the trees you might get a glimpse of Elterwater.

31. **At the fork bear left along the stony path. Again it is signed with occasional yellow arrows. (The right track leads only to the road, which should be visible.) Follow the path as it winds its way round, and go through the kissing gate into the woods.**

☺ There is a lot of undergrowth in the woods, including blackberries, foxgloves and fern-like bracken. It is a popular place with squirrels, who can feed on the many acorns and beech nuts from the trees.

32. **Follow the main path downhill through the woods. At the fork bear left, avoiding the gate off to the right. Follow the path through the trees, leading slightly downhill. (There should now be a small stream down on your right.)**

Q: Soon you should come to a white house. What is it called?

A: 'Bridge Howe'. There is a nameplate on the gate.

33. **After the house there is again a fork. Take either path, both will wind their way downhill towards the river.**

☺ Skelwith Force is visible through the trees ahead. You can pick your way through to have a look, but the walk passes a better viewing point on the opposite bank later on. Take care on the mossy stones.

34. **Whichever path you take, once at the river bear right. (There are many small paths, so if you get lost remember to keep bearing downhill until you see the river, then keep the water on your left.) Follow the main path, which doesn't run closely to the waters edge at all times, but make sure you are always in sight of the river, so as to avoid bearing off deeper into the woods.**

☺ This is the River Brathay, which runs out of Elterwater and into Windermere. It is quite wide at this point, and as you can see there are many trees hanging over the water and keeping it in the shade. Because of this most of the rocks and stones in the water are covered with moss and other small plants, that like shelter and moisture.

35. **Eventually you should come to a wooden kissing gate. Go through this and follow the rocky riverside path. There should now be houses uphill on your right. Cross over the small wooden footbridge.**

☺ If you hear a lot of noise and see flashing lights through the trees on the other side of the river, don't worry, it isn't an alien invasion, it is the workshops of the Kirkstone Slate Gallery. The flashing lights are on the fork-lift trucks. More about the galleries later.

36. **Continue along the riverside path for some way, until the path**

becomes fenced and bears away from the water, leading off to the right. (Do not go though any of the gates on either side, which lead into peoples gardens.) Follow the path around to the road.

37. Taking great care and keeping young children under tight control, cross the road and bear left. (Remember to always walk towards the traffic, so you can see it at all times.) Follow the road around to the left and carefully cross the bridge. There is a stopping point in the middle in case there is traffic coming.

    (Refreshments are available on the left before the bridge, at the Rosewood Tea Gardens, very nice on a sunny day.)

38. Bear left immediately after the bridge and continue upstream, passing the slate tables and chairs of the riverside picnic area. Keep left along the driveway and go through the gate, heading for the Kirkstone Galleries.

☺ On the right of the driveway, near the gate, look out for the large, pointed stones, which are slabs of slate, which is quarried in many areas around the Lake District, including Elterwater, where the walk started. Apart from being used for building houses and walls, it is also made into all kinds of ornaments, as you will see if you take a look around the gallery, but remember to take care where you put your hands, in case you break anything!

Refreshments available at 'Chesters' within the gallery. Seating inside and out. In an emergency, there is a bus back to Elterwater from Skelwith Bridge. The bus stop is on the main road next to the phone box.

39. Pass in front of Chesters and bear left along the rear driveway, passing between the slate workshops. Keep straight ahead and do not stray.

☺ Here you will see men at work cutting pieces from huge slabs of slate, which can then be made into any of the objects on sale in the gallery. Some of the machines are very noisy, and the men have to wear 'headphones' to keep the sound out. They also have to wear 'hard hats' to protect their heads. Look out for a fork-lift truck lifting heavy blocks of stone.

40. Keep straight ahead through the workshops and continue along the shady pathway alongside the river. Keep the river avoiding all paths/gateways to the right which lead only to the road.

41. After a short way the path divides. Either direction will do, as long

as you continue heading upstream. **Various paths and bridges lead to the rocky outcrop that serves as a viewing point for the waterfall.**

☺ This is Skelwith Force, which carries more water than any other waterfall in the Lake District. It is very impressive after heavy rain, when a huge amount of water comes pouring between the cleft in the rocks. Take care near the water. Don't go to near the edge and don't paddle!

42. **Continue along the riverbank. Keep straight ahead, i.e., don't follow the farm trackway up to the road. Go through the kissing gate onto National Trust land. Keep straight ahead towards a knoll of trees. (Might be muddy here in winter or wet weather.)**

☺ Again, there will probably be sheep and cows in this field. The high, rocky fells straight ahead in the distance are the Langdale Pikes, which can be seen from all over the Lake District.

43. **The path soon leads closer to the river. Pass the clump of trees on your right. From here on the path is very easy to follow. After a short way pass through a kissing gate and keep straight ahead towards the lake.**

☺ The river is quite wide here, and there are water-lilies in places. You may see ducks on the water. Ducks 'moult' in the summer, which means they shed some of their feathers, like a dog loses some of its hair in hot weather, so in the summer you may see patches of small, soft feathers that have come off when the duck has been 'preening' itself.

A little further ahead you should come to Elterwater, which is the smallest of the sixteen lakes in the Lake District. It is oddly shaped and most of it is hidden from view. Here there is a shingle beach, which is a nice spot to have a picnic or just a rest and admire, the scenery. 'Elterwater' means 'the lake of the swans'. There are often a pair of swans here, possibly with their young, which are called cygnets Unlike many animals, once swans find a partner they stay together for life.

44. **Go through the kissing gate into the woods. Follow the clear path through the trees, avoiding the path leading off to the right, again this leads only to the road. Keep to the main path at all times.**

☺ Just over half a mile to go now . . .

45. **After some way the path bears round to the left. There should now be fields on your right. Keep ahead along the main path.**

☺ The lake is now over on your left. There are many reeds and other water plants along the edge of the lake, including irises, which have bright yellow flowers at the top of a long stem. These reeds make a suitable place for water birds to build their nests. Apart from swans you might see coots, which are small and black, or herons which have long legs and often stand in the shallow water at the edge of the lake.

46. **Cross the small footbridge, after which the path bears around to the right, and there should now be a stream on your left.**

There is access to the water from various stony 'beaches' along the path. Take care in case the stones are slippery.

☺ Over on the left, over the river, you might be able to see the rest of the lake in the distance. After some way the rooftops of Elterwater village should come into view ahead, which will tell you that you are nearing the end of the walk.

47. **Continue ahead and go through the gate. Keep straight ahead through the National Trust car park and bear right into the village centre.**

Elterwater & The Forces Checklist

- [ ] A sheep with a black head
- [ ] A sheep with a white head
- [ ] A white cottage
- [ ] A wooden gate
- [ ] A brown cow
- [ ] A black and white cow
- [ ] A pink flower
- [ ] A white flower
- [ ] A blue car
- [ ] A bush with prickles
- [ ] A squirrel
- [ ] A rabbit
- [ ] A mountain bike
- [ ] Someone walking with a dog
- [ ] A duck
- [ ] A swan

6. Eskdale

The valley of the River Esk is as picturesque as any valley in Lakeland, and this waterside walk is rewarding in any season. Also of interest is the Ravenglass And Eskdale Railway. For a complete day out park at Ravenglass, get the miniature train to Dalegarth Station in Eskdale, do the walk along the river and return by train to Ravenglass.

Starting point: Dalegarth Station on the Ravenglass & Eskdale Railway. (NY173007). There is a pay and display car park next to the station.

By Rail: The main BR line runs through Ravenglass. From here change to the Ravenglass & Eskdale Railway. Dalegarth station is the end of the line.

Distance: Entire route 3½ miles

Terrain: Riverside paths, mainly gravelled. Relatively flat.

Maps: OS Outdoor leisure 6, OS Pathfinder 89

Public Toilets: Dalegarth station and Ravenglass station

Refreshments: Small café at the station, pub at Boot, (café at Ravenglass station, pubs close by)

☺ **(AT DALEGARTH STATION)** This is the end of the Ravenglass & Eskdale Railway, which is known locally as the 'La'al Ratty' (or 'Little Ratty'). It is the oldest narrow gauge (miniature) railway still running in England. It was built in 1875 to connect nearby mines with the main railway line at Ravenglass, which is a few miles away on the coast. The mines were never very profitable and were closed in 1913.

Metals, such as iron, come from mines. When they are dug up they are mixed with stone. This is called 'ore'. The ore has to be heated to very great temperatures to melt it down, so the metal turns into liquid and can then be poured into moulds. As it cools down it will harden and become solid. Railway tracks are made from metal. Can you think of anything else?

1.   From the station bear left along the lane, passing 'Brook House Hotel' on the left at the crossroads. Here bear right, signed for the church.

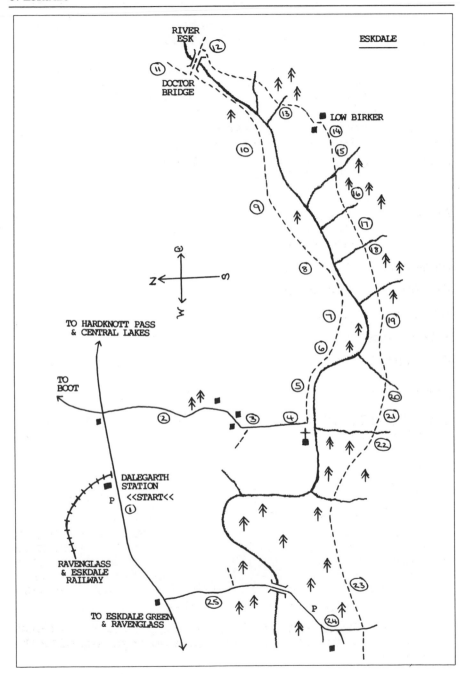

RIVER
ESK

ESKDALE

DOCTOR
BRIDGE

LOW BIRKER

TO HARDKNOTT PASS
& CENTRAL LAKES

TO
BOOT

DALEGARTH
STATION
<<START<<

RAVENGLASS
& ESKDALE
RAILWAY

TO ESKDALE GREEN
& RAVENGLASS

☺ At the crossroads there is a sign pointing off to the left for a place called 'Boot', which might seem an odd name for a village, but it is old English meaning 'the bend in the river'.

Boot is a pleasant stone village, where there is a pub, post office/shop and working water-powered mill, which is open to the public.

☺ **(FURTHER ALONG THE TRACK).** The path now has the familiar drystone walls on both sides, and over them there are fields which might have cows or sheep in them. In a short way look out for the rock-face on the left, which has many bushes and trees growing on it, including rowan, holly and elder. All these trees have berries in the autumn. You have probably seen holly many times. It has prickly leaves and is often used as a decoration at Christmas, but can you recognise the other two? Rowan has bright red berries, and elder has clusters of small black berries and is sometimes made into wine.

2.   Keep to the lower track past the house.

Q: How many chimney pots can you count on the house on the left?

A: There are ten. Five on each side of the roof.

Lone sheep, Eskdale

☺ Soon there is another house on the right, called 'Singleton Kirk House'. 'Kirk' is an old word meaning church, and there is a church a short way further along the lane. In the garden on the right there are several other plants which have berries in the autumn, including rosehips which are like small tomatoes, damsons, which are small purple plums, and blackberries, which grow practically anywhere.

3. **The track winds between drystone walls. Avoid the bridleway off to the right and keep ahead to the church.**

    (Escape route: For a really, really short walk, follow the bridleway and bear right at the end onto the lane, then turn right again for the station).

☺ **(AT THE CHURCH)** This is Saint Catherine's Church. It is made of stone and has two bells on the far side of the roof. Can you see them?

Q: What date is mentioned on the plaque on the church gate?

A: 1937

4. **Continue past the church to the river. Bear left, signed for 'Doctor Bridge'.**

☺ **(AT THE RIVER)** This is the River Esk, which the whole valley, Eskdale, is named after. Here it is wide and clear, and there are many pebbles and rocks. Along the banks there are prickly gorse bushes and another plant which is very common in the Lake District, 'bracken', which is a type of fern.

5. **From the kissing gate take the upper path, signed for "Doctor Bridge". This runs parallel to the river for a short way, but then bears away. Keep left between the drystone walls (not the open gateway) and go through the five bar gate. Continue ahead along the trackway.**

    (Escape route: This will cut nearly 2 miles off the circular route. Go through the kissing gate and bear right along the lower path. Cross the wooden footbridge and bear left along the river. There are many small streams running into the river, and several small, wet caves which should not be entered. Eventually a drystone wall blocks the way ahead. Here bear right, uphill and then right along the gravel path at the top. Continue from Direction 18)

☺ Here the path passes more bracken and colourful rowan trees on the left. In the distance you should be able to see some of the craggy fells that surround Eskdale. Notice how their tops are bare and rocky, and nothing can grow there, while further down there are trees and plants growing.

6. **Follow the path as it leads between bracken and gorse, running above the river.**

☺ Close to the Path there are many dark green gorse bushes, can you spot them? Take care though, they have very sharp prickles. Gorse can have flowers for most of the year, except through the winter. The flowers are yellow and quite strongly scented. There are also occasional trees, like birch and hawthorn.

Down below the river has a row of trees along its banks which hang over the water. It is a very colourful sight in the autumn.

7. **Go through the kissing gate and continue ahead.**

☺ The river is full and fast flowing in wet weather. It collects all the water from the small streams that run down from the surrounding mountain. It joins the sea near Muncaster Castle, which is just a few miles away.

8. **Go through the five bar gate and continue ahead. Avoid all other paths and gateways on either side.**

☺ There may be cows in the fields along the footpath, or perhaps sheep. They may be curious and come towards you to have a good look, but they shouldn't hurt you.

Over on the right you should be able to see a waterfall on the fellside, which has a very long drop and looks spectacular after heavy rain.

9. **Continue ahead at the end of the field, again between drystone walls. There are now fields on both sides. The path soon returns to the riverside. Avoid the permitted path that bears off to the left and continue ahead the river, signed again for 'Doctor Bridge'.**

Escape Route: In an emergency, or to cut the route short so you don't miss the last train, follow the permitted path off to the left, which will eventually bring you to the Eskdale road. Bear left for the station.

10. **After some way you should come to another gate. Go through and continue ahead. (The path is now partially cobbled.)**

☺ Look out for the large rock on the left with moss and grasses growing on it. Moss is a moisture loving plant, but it can survive with very little water when it has to. In hot weather it dries out and waits for the rain to come, which it then soaks up and comes back to life. There is also ivy on the rock. Ivy is a climbing plant. It has 'suckers' which it uses to attach itself to trees, rocks and walls.

11. **Bear right over the bridge.**

(Escape Route: In an emergency bear left, which will take you to the main Eskdale road. The station is just under a mile to the left.)

☺ **(AT THE BRIDGE)** This is called 'Doctor Bridge' and as you can see it has a stone arch over the waters of the River Esk. If you stand on the bridge and look over at the river, you will see that on one side the water flows very fast over rocks. These are called 'rapids'. On the other side the water is very deep, like a swimming pool. The water often looks very green and inviting, but be warned if you decide to paddle: it's very cold!

12. **Bear right after the bridge along trackway signed for 'Dalegarth'. After a short way across the cattle grid and continue along the driveway, which begins to wind uphill.**

☺ On the left is an area of woodland. The trees are quite close together and have tall, thin trunks. On the ground there are many rocks that have fallen down from the high fells. Several streams pass under the trackway on their way to join the river.

13. **Soon a house should come into view. Keep with the main track as it winds between outbuildings and passes the front of the house (Low Birker).**

Q: How many upstairs windows are there are the front of the house?
A: Two.

14. **The track leads slightly uphill after the house and bears around to the right between drystone walls, soon leading downhill.**

☺ On the right there are views over fields down to the river and along the path on the opposite shore which you walked along earlier.

15. **Continue downhill to the ford and cross the stream via the wooden footbridge.**

☺ **(AT THE STREAM)** The track crosses the stream by a 'ford', which is an area where the ground is flat and the water is shallow enough for vehicles to cross in safety. Horses and carts would have come over here and it saved the farmer the trouble of building a bridge, although a wooden footbridge has recently been built, so walkers, like you, can cross without getting their feet wet!

16. **Go through the five bar gate and continue ahead through the bracken.**

☺ On the left you should see the bottom of a high rocky fell, partly covered with bracken. Soon after there is an area of conifers. Keep a look out on the ground for fir-cones.

Q: What is a 'conifer'?

A: A conifer is a tree that has pointed needles instead of flat leaves. Look at these trees. They have tall, straight trunks and dark green needles. Most conifers are 'evergreens' , which means they do not lose their leaves in the winter. Can you tell which trees are evergreens and which are not?

☺ Through the trees there is a small pond which has 'lilies' growing in it. In the spring and summer you should be able to see the large round leaves, or 'lily pads' floating on the surface of the water. Also keep a look out for toadstools beneath the trees, and remember never to touch wild toadstools, mushrooms or berries, as many of them may be poisonous, no matter how nice they look.

17. **After the pond continue straight ahead. Do not go through the open gateway on the right. The track bears to the left of the drystone wall and crosses several small streams.**

18. **Continue ahead along the stony path through the trees. The river should be on your far right, just out of sight.**

Q: In the woods there are mixed trees, including oak, birch and beech. Do you know which of these trees acorns come from?

A: Oak. If it is late summer or autumn you will probably see lots of acorns on the ground. Perhaps you will see squirrels in the woods. They collect acorns to eat through the cold winter months. They hide them to keep them safe, but often forget where.

☺ Between the trees there are many stones and boulders which have moss growing on them. Again look out for mushrooms, which can often be found growing beneath birch trees. Birches have thin, whitish trunks. See if you can spot any.

19. **Cross the stile or go through the five bar gate and continue ahead. (The path now becomes wide and grassy.)**

☺ Further ahead there are fewer trees, and again there is bracken and many prickly gorse bushes.

20. **Other paths join from the left, but keep straight ahead. A drystone wall starts on the right. Bear right with the wall for a short way, but at the crossroads of paths bear left between gorse bushes, leading downhill to a further ford.**

21. **At the ford there are enough stones to use as stepping stones. Follow the track straight ahead.**

☺ There might be sheep grazing between the bracken, so don't be startled if something darts off through the undergrowth. You can probably hear the rushing sound of the river, which runs very fast over rocks at this point.

22. **Keep ahead and go through the five bar gate into the woods. Follow the gravel path through the trees and cross the wooden footbridge. Continue along the path up to a further five bar gate and keep straight ahead.**

☺ This small field is surrounded by woodland. It often has sheep or cows in it, which feed on the grass.

Q: What is a young cow called?
A: A calf.

23. **At the end of the field go through the gate onto the trackway and bear right, leading slightly downhill. Keep to the main track as it leads between drystone walls.**

Q: The house on the left is called Dalegarth Hall. It has several tall chimneys. How many?

A: Five

24. **Follow the track around to the right, avoiding the drive off to the left to the Hall. (In a short way you should pass on the right Trough House Bridge car park). Continue ahead and cross the bridge over the river.**

There is public access to the river at this point.

☺ If you stand on the bridge and look over at the river, you will see again that on one side there are rapids, and on the other the water is deep and clear.

25. **Follow the lane uphill at first, leading through the trees. At the top bear right, which will take you in a short way back to Dalegarth station and the car park.**

Eskdale Checklist

☐ A church bell

☐ A wooden bridge

☐ A stone bridge

☐ A sheep

☐ A waterfall

☐ A wooden gate

☐ A prickly gorse bush

☐ Red berries

☐ A cow

☐ A fir-cone

☐ An acorn

☐ Someone with a dog

7. Finsthwaite

This short walk is designed to fit in with a ride on the Lakeside and Haverthwaite Steam Railway. The Windermere Steamers also leave from Lakeside, so a full day of walking and varied transport can be arranged from this one location. Please check all train and boat times in advance, either at a T.I.C. or by phoning: 015395-31188.

Starting Point: Either: start at Newby Bridge halt. From Newby Bridge take the bridge over the river and take the first left turning, signed for Finsthwaite and Rusland. There is limited parking along the roadside running parallel to the river. Continue along the lane on foot for a short way to the station to begin the walk. Or, park at Lakeside, well signed for 'Lakeside Steamers and L & H Railway', along a driveway next to the Lakeside Hotel. There is a large pay and display car park here. Catch the train to Newby Bridge, do the walk, then catch the train back again.

By Bus: Services to Newby Bridge from Ambleside, Windermere station & Bowness.

Distance: 2 miles

Terrain: Footpaths for most of the way, some uphill stretches. Short distances along quiet lanes.

Maps: OS Landranger 97

Public Toilets: Lakeside

Refreshments: Lakeside

☺ (AT NEWBY BRIDGE HALT) This station has been set up as it would have looked at the turn of the century, a hundred years ago, when the line ran a lot further than it does today, which is now just 3½ miles.

Q: How many feet above sea level is Newby Bridge Halt?
A: 151. Look for the sign.

☺ You can see over the lines a craggy rock face, which was cut through to make the railway line. This is called a 'cutting'. You may have noticed when you've been on a train that the tracks

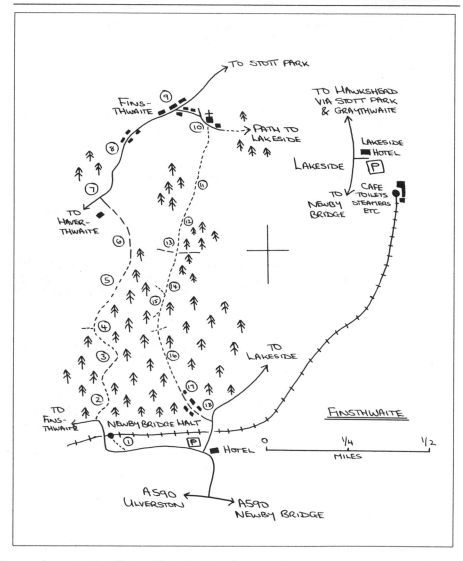

have to be flat, which is why they go through so many tunnels or over viaducts if they have to cross a valley.

Q: In which year did the Lakeside & Haverthwaite Railway open as it is today?

A: 1973. There is a plaque on the platform to commemorate the opening on 2nd May that year.

1. **Leave the platform via any of the gates and bear right along the lane, leading slightly uphill. The railway should be down on your right. Bear right across the bridge, and take the public bridleway on the immediate right after the bridge, signed for Finsthwaite.**

☺ This is a stony trackway leading uphill through the woods, where there are many wild flowers in the spring and summer. There are many different types of tree, including oak, sycamore, lime and holly. How many can you recognise?

2. **Keep to the main path leading uphill.**

☺ This is a bridleway, which means it can be used for horses and also cycles, so you might see hoof prints or tyre tracks on the ground.

There are many different birds here, which you will probably be able to hear in the summer months, singing in the treetops or hopping about in the undergrowth. Sparrows and blackbirds are quite common, and in the early mornings you might hear a woodpecker, pecking at the tree trunks.

3. **The path continues steadily uphill and soon bears around quite sharply to the left. Avoid all other minor paths into the woods.**

☺ You may see around you that some trees have been cut down or 'felled'. Some trees might be marked for felling, and might have a circle or line painted on them. Any trees that are old or dead are cut down, to stop them falling on anyone. Look out for tree stumps. Many older tree stumps may have moss, fungus or small ferns growing on them.

4. **Do not go through the gate signed as a footpath. Keep to the trackway, now with a drystone wall running on your left.**

Q: If you look over on the left there are grassy fields, probably with cows or sheep in them. Can you see the house in the distance? How many chimneys has it got?

A: Two. One at each end of the roof.

☺ There are many different types of trees in the wood, including oak, birch, sycamore and beech. Of these four types of trees, one has silvery bark, one produces acorns, one produces 'keys' or 'helicopters', with seeds inside, and one produces nuts in prickly casings, which squirrels like to eat. But do you know which?

Oak trees produce acorns in the autumn. These are the seeds of the tree, from which a new tree could grow. Birch trees have silvery bark. Sycamore trees produce 'keys'. Beech trees produce beech nuts, which have its seeds inside. The prickly casing is to protect the seeds.

5. **Go through the gate barring the main path and continue ahead, with the drystone wall still on your left.**

☺ There are several rhododendron bushes in the woods over on the left. They have dark green, oval leaves, which do not fall off in the winter. In the spring they have large colourful flowers. The flowers on these rhododendrons are pink and lilac.

There are often bees buzzing around flowers, such as rhododendrons. The bees collect 'pollen' from the flowers, which they make into honey.

6. **Go through a further gate and join a farm driveway, with farm buildings on your left.**

☺ On the right are small grassy fields with drystone walls. Again, these will probably have cows or sheep grazing in them.

Growing close to the high stone wall on the left are lots of tall plants with bluish-purple flowers in the summer, which seem to be very popular with butterflies.

7. **Bear right along the quiet lane.**

☺ Along the sides of the lane there are many wild plants, like dandelions, blackberries and ferns. Dandelions are very common, and you will recognise their yellow flower from gardens or parks. The white round dandelion 'clocks', as they are often called, are the seeds of the plant. If you blow on them the seeds will scatter and float away in the wind. Blackberries have their seeds inside the fruit. These are then eaten by birds and other animals (including people) and will eventually get back to the soil in the animals droppings. The seeds of ferns are arranged in rows on the backs of the leaves.

You should soon be able to see the small spire of a church over on the right.

8. Pass houses as the road enters the village of Finsthwaite.

☺ This is the village of Finsthwaite. There are many villages in Lakeland with the word 'thwaite' in their name. It means 'clearing'. Most of the area was at one tine covered with thick forests, so each family group would cut down enough trees to make a clearing in which they could grow crops.

9. The first right turning is a cul-de-sac, but take the second (opposite the post box) leading slightly downhill towards the spire of the church.

☺ The church is called St Peter's of Finsthwaite. It has a 'lychgate' which is the sort of porch over the gates into the churchyard. Many churches have these. It was where the coffins would be left until the vicar arrived to carry out the funeral.

In the tower of the church there are bells which chime every quarter of an hour.

10. Take the lane to the right of the church, signed as a dead end and take the footpath off to the right, signed for Newby Bridge. Follow the path straight across the field, which soon starts to lead slightly uphill.

☺ This is an open, grassy field, where there are often sheep grazing. See if you can find any clumps of their wool in the grass.

Q: What is a female sheep called?
A: A 'ewe'. A male is called a 'ram'.

☺ Over on the right you should be able to see the houses of the village, and might be able to make out the lane you walked along to get here.

11. At the top end of the field there is a gate in the drystone with a set of steps leading over. Climb this, cross the stream beyond and continue ahead.

☺ The path is still slightly uphill, but isn't too difficult. Looking behind you, you should be able to see the pointed spire of the little church, and in the background the high fells in the middle of the Lake District. In the winter these mountains will most probably have snow on their peaks.

12. **Keep straight ahead. There should now be an area, of walled/fenced woodland on your immediate left.**

☺ There are often cows in this field, hard at work eating grass. You often see old baths in fields which are used to hold water for cows, who can drink a lot every day. Chewing grass is obviously very thirsty work! On summer days the cows flick their long tails to keep flies away from them.

There is an area of marsh over on the right. Notice the tall, pointed grass, which is a type of water-loving reed. If you ever see reeds like this it should tell you that the ground is probably water-logged, so watch where you're treading, or you'll get wet feet.

13. **Cross the raised trackway leading into the woods. (Do not go into the woods at this point: they are private.) Continue straight ahead to the end of the field, where there is a set of steps over the drystone wall marked with a yellow arrow. (The steps are difficult to see at a distance.) Cross over into the woods and bear left along the narrow pathway.**

☺ Again these woods have many different types of trees, but they are mainly oaks. Even in winter, when the trees are bare, you should be able to tell from the leaves on the ground, and also there might be acorns which haven't yet been found and hidden away by the squirrels. You might be able to smell a strong onion-like smell at certain points. This is from a plant called 'wood garlic' which can often be found in damp woods. It has long green leaves and white flowers in the summer.

14. **Cross the small stream and continue ahead between the trees. After a short way the path splits. Keep left along the narrow path leading slightly uphill. Keep straight ahead and avoid the paths off to either side.**

☺ There is a lot of bracken between the trees, and also rocks with moss growing on them. In the treetops there will probably be many birds singing. Look out for sparrows (small brown birds), crows (all black) and magpies (black and white, usually seen in pairs). If it is autumn or winter and there are few leaves on the trees you might be able to see their nests high up in the branches.

15. **A short way the path goes through a gap in a crumbling drystone wall and soon starts to bear downhill. Keep along the main path.**

☺ You may be pleased to hear it's downhill all the way now! You might be able to hear cars on the main road at Newby Bridge, or you might hear the steam train.

16. **Follow the path winding quite steeply downhill. At the bottom climb the stile next to the gate and follow the trackway.**

Q: On the left there is a house with two chimneys. What is its name? (Look for the main gate to the house to find the answer.)

A: 'Dove Cottage'. A dove is a type of pigeon, usually all white.

17. **Keep straight ahead, passing between garages and further houses. Avoid the path off to the left and continue to the road.**

☺ You should soon be able to see the steam railway on your right. If you're lucky you might see a train going past.

18. **Bear right along the road and cross the railway bridge. Take the first right turning for the car park, or continue a short way along the lane to return to Newby Bridge Halt.**

Boats on Windermere, Lakeside

Q: What is the name of the hotel at the corner?
A: The 'Swan Hotel'.

Lakeside is well worth a visit if you haven't come from there by the
train. It is only a short way by car. Return to the junction and bear left.
It is well-signed. There, apart from the start of the steam railway, you
will find boat trips, a museum and a café looking over Windermere.

Finsthwaite checklist

- [ ] A steam train
- [ ] Pink flowers (in spring or summer)
- [ ] A bush with prickles
- [ ] A white house
- [ ] A stone bridge
- [ ] A tree stump
- [ ] A seagull
- [ ] An acorn (in autumn or winter)
- [ ] A horse
- [ ] A cow
- [ ] A duck or swan
- [ ] a spiders web

8. Grasmere and Rydal Water

Grasmere is right in the heart of Lakeland, and is, of course, renowned as the home of the poet, William Wordsworth. Because of its literary connections, the area is very popular, but never so busy that a day out is ruined. The scenery is spectacular, and the short climbs afford excellent views over the two lakes. It's no wonder Wordsworth chose this place for his home, and was so inspired by his surroundings. The walk is short enough for half a day, but if you can afford the time, spend longer.

Starting Point: White Moss Common, off the A591 Keswick to Ambleside road, between the lakes of Grasmere and Rydal Water. (NY350065). Car parks on both sides of the main road.

By Bus: A regular bus service operates from Windermere via Ambleside, and from Keswick. Ask for White Moss Common.

Distance: Entire route 5½ miles. Rydal Water only - 3 miles. Grasmere only - 3½ miles (from the car park follow the paths through the common to the bridge over the River Rothay. Cross the bridge and take the main path straight ahead, leading uphill through the woods to a narrow gate in a drystone wall. Go through and bear right, then continue with direction 12).

Public Toilets: Main car park, White Moss Common (south of the main road).

Refreshments: Tea-room at Rydal Hall, Rydal. Seats inside and out. Cafés in Grasmere nearby.

Pushchairs: The route is unsuitable for pushchairs, though there are good, flat paths around White Moss Common which are ideal for a short walk.

1. **Start on the main road. Between the car parks there is a footpath (heading north) with a post box on the left and a house, 'the Coach House' on the right. Follow the stony path as it leads uphill.**

Q: What large letters can you see on the front of the post box, and What do you think they mean?

A: E II R, which stands for Elizabeth Regina. This means Queen Elizabeth the Second, because the post box was put up while

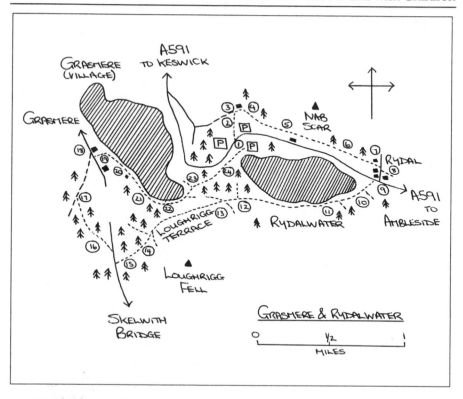

the present Queen was on the throne. Keep a look out for any other post boxes and see what letters they have on them.

2.   **Continue along the stony trackway, passing a waterfall on the left. Keep right along main path, leading uphill.**

☺ **(AT THE WATERFALL)** Look at the way the water pours over the rock and falls into the pool far below. After heavy rain there will be a great amount of water coming down from the mountains heading towards the lakes. Notice all the mosses and ferns which grow near to the water because they like the damp soil and atmosphere.

(FURTHER UPHILL) There are many different types of tree along the pathway, including oak, beach, sycamore and birch. You might have one of these trees near your home or in your garden. See if you can recognise any.

3.   **Go through the five bar gate ahead, not the gate to the right. At the top bear right along a public bridleway._**

(To the right are views over Rydal Water to Loughrigg Fell.)

4.   **Go through a further gate and continue along the trackway. It becomes craggy underfoot in some places, but is not difficult. Keep the drystone wall on your right and do not stray from the main path onto quarrying scars on the left as this is dangerous.**

☺ This rocky hill is called Nab Scar. There is a tunnel running through its middle carrying water from the Thirlmere reservoir nearby, nearly 100 miles to Manchester, where it is piped into peoples' homes. No trace of the tunnel can be seen at all.

5.   **At one point the main path bears away from the wall, but rejoins it soon after. Go through a further gate and follow the path ahead.**

(There are further views across Rydal Water to Loughrigg Fell.)

☺ If you look over the lake you may be able to see the entrance to a large cave. It isn't really a cave at all, as caves are natural.

Looking out of Rydal Cave towards Nab Scar

This is a mine, and at one time slate was cut from here, as it was in many parts of the area. The mine has been closed a long time and all that remains is this gaping hole in the hillside. It is said that everyone from the nearby town of Ambleside could easily fit into the mine at once. (i.e. it's quite big!)

Q: Keep a look out for the stone seat beside the pathway. What initials are carved on the backrest?

A: GBG

6. **The path soon begins to lead downhill. Go through the gate and continue between the drystone walls.**

☺ Look for the tree on the left and see how its roots are clinging to the wall for support. Over the years they have grown around the rocks and stones in search of water. A tree feeds through its roots and also needs sunlight on its leaves to grow.

7. **At the road bear right, downhill.**

☺ **(AT RYDAL MOUNT: FIRST HOUSE ON THE RIGHT)** This was the last home of the poet, William Wordsworth, where he lived for many years with his wife and sister and where he died at the age of eighty.

Rydal Mount is now open to the public daily from March to October. It's an interesting house with attractive grounds but probably not really suited to most children.

On the left of the lane is a driveway leading behind Rydal Hall, where a small tea-room can be found next to the Rydal Falls. The gardens to the hall are also open to the public daily. Free admission, but donations welcome.

8. **From Rydal Mount continue down the lane towards the main road.**

Q: Does the church have a tower or steeple?

A: Tower.

(A short detour through the churchyard will take you to the National Trust owned "Dora's Field", once owned by Wordsworth, named after his daughter. It is a pleasant piece of woodland, well worth a visit in spring to see all the daffodils planted by the Wordsworths.)

9. **Bear right along the main road. Carefully cross the road opposite the 'Badger Bar' and cross the wooden bridge over the River Rothay. Bear right towards Rydal Water.**

😊 There are often horses in this field grazing. On the river or the lake you might see ducks, swans or even seagulls.

10. **Follow the path past the foot of the lake and go through the kissing gate into the woods. Follow the path through the woods and emerge beside Rydal Water. Take the lower path along the lake shore.**

😊 If you look across the water, you might be able to see people on the path that you walked along earlier.

The lake has two main islands. On one of them are the remains of a summer house. The ruins are still there, but are very hard to see. Can you spot them?

11. **Clamber over the rocky outcrop that juts into the water and continue along the path. It soon rises and bears away from the lake and follows the course of a drystone wall on the right. Pass the derelict barn, visible on the right, and keep the drystone wall to your right. The path rises towards the woods of White Moss Common.**

Escape Route: To return to the car parks, go through a kissing gate in the wall on the right and follow the path downhill through the woods. Keep to the main path and cross the footbridge over the River Rothay. Bear right along the main pathway for the car park.

12. **Continue along the path with the drystone wall on your right. Ahead is a crossroads of paths. To the left is a bench looking back towards Rydal Water. To the right is a path downhill to Grasmere Lake. Keep to the central pathway, leading uphill to Loughrigg Terrace.**

😊 **(ON THE LEFT)** This is Loughrigg Fell. You can see heaps of slate in places along its slopes which are left from the days of the quarry.

Q: On both sides of the path are trees with prickles. Do you know what these trees are called?

A: Hawthorns. They have white or pink flowers in spring and red berries in the autumn.

13. **Continue along the terrace. In wet weather several small streams may cross the path.**

☺ From here you have a good view over Grasmere Lake towards the village. Behind the village is a hill with a rocky top, known as the 'Lion and the Lambs' because some of the rocks form the shape of a lion with a lamb between its paws. See if you can make out the shapes.

14. **Towards the end of the terrace a path veers uphill to the summit of Loughrigg, (for those that still have plenty of energy to spare and wish to make a detour) but keep straight ahead, crossing a small stream and continuing into the trees. Go through an iron kissing gate and keep to the main pathway.**

    Escape Route: To cut a mile off the journey bear right through the gate and follow the path down through Red Bank. Bear right at the cottage along a path signed for the lake. Bear right along the water's edge and continue from Direction 22.

15. **When the path splits keep right and climb up to the road, bear right. Take great care and look out for oncoming vehicles. It is only a very short way along the road, then take the footpath leading off to the left. Do not go up the steps, but follow the path downhill between ferns and foxgloves.**

Q: You should pass a metal bench on your left. What does it say on to back of the bench?

A: Lake District Association.

16. **Go through the kissing gate into Redbank Woods and follow the path.**

☺ Little light can get through the branches and leaves to shine on the ground in the woods so there is no grass and few plants. There may be fallen branches and dead leaves on the floor of the woods. These will rot down and nourish the soil, and that way feed the trees that continue to grow here.

Keep a look-out for wildlife, such as rabbits and squirrels.

17. **Go through the kissing gate at the end of the woods, and bear right downhill along the trackway. In places the track becomes craggy underfoot. Continue to the road, then bear right.**

Q: In the wall opposite is another post box. What are the letters on the front?

A: VR for Victoria Regina - Queen Victoria. This post box is much older than the one near the car park.

18. **Follow the road for a short way, then take the permitted path to the lake shore on the left through a gap in the drystone wall, with a set of wooden steps leading down.**

Q: These wooden steps were placed here in memory of someone who died in 1984. When was this person born?

A: 1920.

19. **At the shore bear right and continue along the path alongside the lake.**

☺ Grasmere has one island, which you can see in the middle of the lake. There are often rowing boats on the water as well as ducks and swans.

20. **Pass behind the boat-house and continue.**

Q: **(AT THE BOAT-HOUSE)** What do you think this building is for?

A: It's a boat-house, where boats are kept.

21. **Go through the gate into the woods. Keep close to the water and pass through a further gate at the end of the woods to emerge on a shingle "beach" at the foot of Loughrigg Fell.**

This is a popular spot to stop and admire the view and to paddle.

22. **Continue past the "beach" and cross the footbridge over the river.**

☺ Water flows from Grasmere over the weir (a type of waterfall) and flows into Rydal Water, and from there it flows into Windermere, the largest of the Lakes.

23. **Go up the steps into the woods. The path soon descends to a gate. Continue through the gate and follow the path along the river.**

☺ **(AFTER THE GATE)** New trees have been planted here, with wooden fences around them. This is to protect them from wild animals, who might eat their young bark and damage the tree.

As the tree gets bigger the bark becomes harder and the tree will no longer need protecting.

24. **Go through a further gate and bear left, away from the river and footbridge. Follow the path back to the car park.**

Grasmere and Rydal Water Checklist

☐ A moss covered tree trunk

☐ Someone on a mountain bike

☐ Ivy growing on a wall

☐ A stained glass window

☐ Someone with a rucksack

☐ A foxglove

☐ A round chimney

☐ A bird's feather

☐ A cow

☐ A duck

9. Great Langdale

Great Langdale is a mecca for walkers and climbers lured by the impressive and unmistakable profile of the Langdale Pikes. Apart from the well-trodden routes that lead to the high ground, there are various paths and tracks along the floor of this popular valley which make for excellent family walking. The only drawback is that Great Langdale's attractions make it busy at the best of times and hectic at the weekend, but only for the car driver. Once on foot it only takes a few minutes to get away from the car parks and the crowds.

This route is a figure-of-eight, so it can easily be split in two.

Starting Point:	The Old Dungeon Ghyll Hotel (NY286061). There is a National Trust car park next to the hotel. From Ambleside follow the A593, and bear right at Skelwith Bridge along the B5343, signed for Elterwater & Great Langdale. Alternatively, if the car park is full, there is further parking at the National Trust's Stickle Ghyll car park, half a mile back down the road. Start the route from Direction 7
By Bus:	Service from Ambleside into Great Langdale, stopping at the Old Dungeon Ghyll Hotel
Distance:	4 miles
Terrain:	A few slight climbs along stony paths.
Maps:	OS Outdoor Leisure 6. OS Landranger 90
Public Toilets:	At the back of the National Trust's Stickle Ghyll Car Park, on the right
Refreshments:	The Stickle Barn: pub, café etc, with seats outside

1. **From the front of the hotel follow the driveway back towards the road. (The car parks should be over on your left.) At the junction of driveways, bear left towards the bridge, but go through the wooden five bar gate on your left almost immediately: i.e. before you have crossed the bridge. (This gate is currently unsigned.)**

2. **Head straight across the field.**

☺ This valley is called Great Langdale, and it is right in the very middle of the Lake District. The stream which flows over on your

right is called Great
Langdale Beck, and
it collects water from
all the surrounding
fells and valleys and
takes it into the lake
at Elterwater.

3. **At the end of the field
    go through the five
    bar gate and con-
    tinue straight ahead.
    There should be a
    grassy hillock on
    your left, and a clear
    path winds its way
    around its lower
    slopes. Continue
    straight ahead, pass-
    ing an open gateway
    in a drystone wall.**

☺ There may be sheep
   in any of these
   grassy fields, so look
   for some tufts of their
   wool on the ground.

4. **Head for the far right
    corner of the field.
    Avoid the bridge
    leading over the
    beck,   continue
    ahead. There are oc-
    casional direction
    arrows. Cross over
    the stile onto the
    riverbank. Bear left
    and cross a further
    stile. Keep ahead
    with the river over
    on your right.**

☺ There   are   many

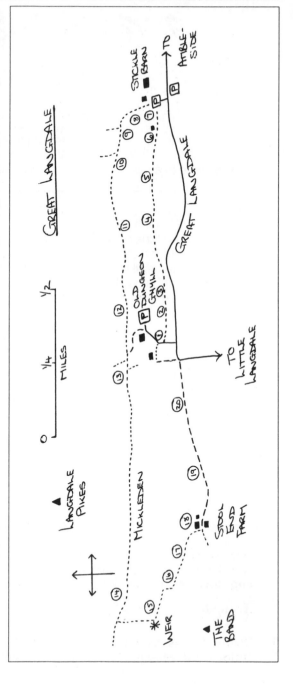

plants growing amongst the grass, including stinging nettles, prickly thistles and buttercups. You may now be able to hear the sound of a waterfall.

5. **After a short way, bear right over the bridge and cross the stile on the left. Follow the clear rutted trackway leading ahead.**

☺ The fell on the right is called 'Lingmoor'. 'Ling' is an old word for heather, which covers the top of the fell.

Q: You should soon pass a house on the left, which is surrounded by many different types of tree, including hawthorn, sycamore and holly. Which of these three types of tree do NOT have red berries in the autumn?

A: Sycamore.

6. **Keep straight ahead, crossing over the driveway of the cottage. Continue to a five bar gate in the drystone wall opposite, which will lead you into the National Trust's Stickle Ghyll Car Park. Bear left.**

(Public Toilets can be found towards the back of the car park, on the right. Also there is a shelter with benches and information point. A gate on the right leads through to the Stickle Barn for those requiring refreshments.)

7. **Head towards the back of the car park. Pass the toilets on the right and continue along the stony trackway with a drystone wall on your right, and an area of woodland on the left. Go through the gate and continue to a further gateway. Follow the clear pathway leading uphill.**

☺ You should be able to hear the roar of the waterfalls, bringing all the water down from the Langdale Pikes above. This is a very popular area for walking, and there are probably several walkers with rucksacks heading up the steep paths to the top of the Pikes. The water from here eventually join the River Brathay and empties into Windermere, which is the longest lake in England at 10½ miles long. At the other end of the lake the water heads out to join the sea.

8. **Bear left and continue uphill passing between fenced areas of trees. Bear left again along the rocky path, now heading away**

from the stream. There should now be a drystone wall on your left.

☺ In wet weather there may be several small streams running over the path. If you look you should have a view along the valley of Great Langdale, with its green fields along the beck.

9. Continue uphill over rocks to a kissing gate straight ahead, not the one leading off to the left. Follow the path downhill, with a wall on your left.

☺ At the falls there are several shallow pools which are excellent for paddling, but remember that wet rocks can be slippery, so take care and never play in or near water without asking an adult. Notice how the holly bushes hang over the water. Perhaps some of them have red berries on them. These can be eaten by birds and other small animals, but don't try eating them yourself as many wild fruits and berries can be poisonous to people.

10. Cross the wooden bridge, then keep left, with the drystone wall on your left. Keep straight ahead and avoid all gates to the left.

☺ If you look ahead you should be able to see there are lots of trees in the valley, but higher up the trees thin out, and at the very tops of the fells there are no trees at all, only bracken and heather. At one time, thousands of years ago, the whole of the Lake District was covered with trees, all except for the highest rocky peaks of the mountains where nothing could grow. Our ancestors began chopping and burning the trees, at first for wood to built houses and later to clear land for farming. Now there are very few areas left covered with trees.

11. After some way go through the gate and continue ahead, leading uphill at first.

☺ Notice the stone barn to the right of the path, in which sheep can shelter in bad weather. Perhaps there are sheep in it now. If so, take care not to startle them.

Q: Here's an easy one. What is a baby sheep called?
A: A lamb.

12. Continue ahead, passing the white house and go through the gate. Follow the path downhill and bear right along the track. Avoid

all gates, which will lead you astray. Keep the drystone wall on
your left.

🙂 As you get closer to the 'head' or beginning of the valley the path
gets flatter. There is a farm over on the left surrounded by walled
fields which might have cows, sheep or horses in them.

13. **Go through the gate and keep to the lower path. Go through a
further gate and keep with that trusty drystone wall.**

🙂 Up on the right you should have a good view up to the rocky tops
of the Langdale Pikes, which can be seen from miles away. From
the top of the Pikes there are views all over the Lake District.
There are often people rock climbing in this area. They tend to
wear bright colours like orange or yellow, so they can easily be
seen, in case they get into trouble. Several thousand years ago,
the people who lived in the valley set up an axe factory close to
here, and made axe heads from a very hard type of stone which
was quarried from the Pikes above. Axes from here have been
found all over the world.

14. **After some way bear left with the wall and follow the path over
the grass to the stream. Cross via the wooden bridge.**

🙂 There are often sheep roaming freely here, so keep your dog on
a lead if you have one. It isn't unusual to see the sheep walking
in single file across the bridge, or paddling through a shallow part
of the stream.

This is now the valley of Mickleden. If you look over to the right
you should be able to see the very head of the valley, which
climbs up to the high fells. These are among the highest
mountains in England.

15. **Bear left after the bridge. The path follows the stream for a very
short way, then winds uphill slightly and begins to lead away.
Soon there should be a drystone wall on your left. Ahead, in the
distance you should be able to see the roofs of farm buildings,
which is where you're heading.**

16. **After a short way there are drystone walls on both sides, and a
clear rutted trackway to follow. This soon leads through a gate
onto private land. At this point bear to the right, well-signed, still
between the drystone walls.**

☺ On the side of the fell ahead there are small groups of evergreen trees, which do not lose their leaves in the winter. This area is surrounded by high, rocky fells, which are very popular with walkers and climbers. sometimes people get into trouble and the Mountain Rescue Helicopter has to come out to take them to safety. The helicopter can often be seen on patrol along the valley.

17. After a short way bear left and go through the gate. Follow the clear path ahead towards the farm.

☺ Again there will probably be sheep grazing close to the path, but look out also for cows, horses and goats.

Q: Do you know what a male and female goat are called?

A: A male is a Billy Goat. The female is a Nanny Goat.

18. Pass the back of the farmhouse and go through the five bar gate marked 'path' which leads into the farmyard. Bear right along the driveway between barns.

Q: How many chimneys can you count on the farmhouse?

The footbridge, Mickleden

A: Five.

☺ Look out for hens and sheep dogs in the farm yard.

19. **Follow the driveway between grassy fields, crossing over a cattle grid after a short way.**

☺ The driveway soon crosses over a wide stream, which again brings water down from the high fells. It joins the stream you crossed earlier and eventually leads through Elterwater and into Windermere.

Over on the left there are good views of the Langdale Pikes, and also back into the head of Mickleden.

20. **Cross a further cattle grid and follow the drive to the lane. Bear left and cross the arched stone bridge across the beck. Go through the gate and bear right and go through the kissing gate onto the driveway. The turning almost directly opposite leads back to the hotel, bus stops and car park.**

Great Langdale Checklist

☐ A wooden bridge

☐ A sheep with a white head

☐ A cow

☐ A white house

☐ A rock climber

☐ A hen

☐ Someone with a camera

☐ A stone bridge

☐ A sheep with a black head

☐ A horse

☐ A pink flower

☐ A mountain rescue helicopter

☐ A tent

☐ Someone with a rucksack

10. Grizedale

Quite understandably, Grizedale is one of the best-known and most popular of all the Cumbrian forests. It is an ideal place for the family, where there is something for everyone, including an adventure playground, mountain bike hire, sculptures at various locations throughout the forest, some of which are of great interest to children, and of course there is no shortage of wildlife.

The visitor centre has toilets, refreshments, free displays relating to nature and forest management, and also a gift shop where you can buy detailed maps of the forest showing the location of the sculptures and all the various paths and trackways.

Grizedale is a working forest and certain areas may on occasion be closed due to felling. Otherwise the forest is open at all times.

Starting Point:	Grizedale Visitor Centre (SD336944). Grizedale is well-signed from Hawkshead. Alternatively, the Moor Top car park (SD343965). Begin at direction 12.
By Bus:	Services from Ambleside & Hawkshead to the Visitor Centre
Distance:	5 miles
Terrain:	Good forest trackways for most of the route. Rocky paths in places. Some brief climbs, though the majority of the route is fairly level.
Maps:	OS Outdoor Leisure 7, OS Landranger 97
Public Toilets:	Grizedale Forest Centre
Refreshments:	Grizedale Forest Centre
Pushchairs:	From Moor Top to the visitor centre (2½ miles) is suitable for pushchairs. Return the same way. For a short walk from the visitor centre the Ridding Wood Trail is ideal. Begin at Direction 1 and use the pushchair route to return.

There is a multimedia display in the visitor centre depicting the history of the forest, its wildlife and the story of timber production. There are computer games to test your forestry and natural history knowledge. Also toilets, tearoom and gallery.

1.   **From the visitor centre (with the shop on your left and the café on your right) continue ahead to the road. Bear right for a short way,**

taking great care, then cross over to the left into the car park, following signs for the 'Ridding Wood Trail' at the back of the car park. Pass the campsite shop on the left, and follow the blue and white topped posts.

☺ You might notice in the car park that there are *low* walls which are all that remain of Grizedale Hall, which once stood here. During the Second World War it was used as a Prisoner Of War Camp, where German soldiers were held. There were eight look out towers built, so that guards had a good view over the grounds of the hall to make sure none of the prisoners escaped. Instead of searchlights they used car headlights at night. The old hall has since been pulled down.

On the right there is a campsite where there are probably many tents and caravans. In the spring there are hundreds of daffodils along the pathway and throughout this part of the forest. Look out for a boar in the bushes on the left of the path. A boar is a wild pig, and there were once many living in this area, in fact 'Grizedale' means 'the valley of the wild boar'.

2. **The main path goes round to the right and into the woods. Keep to the upper path.**

☺ There are many interesting sculptures here, including a wooden xylophone, which you can have a go on. Pick a simple tune, like a nursery rhyme, and see if you can play it. If you look down to the right, towards the campsite, you should be able to see some carvings of deer standing on the roof of an old barn.

'Waiting for Lunch' – wooden sculpture

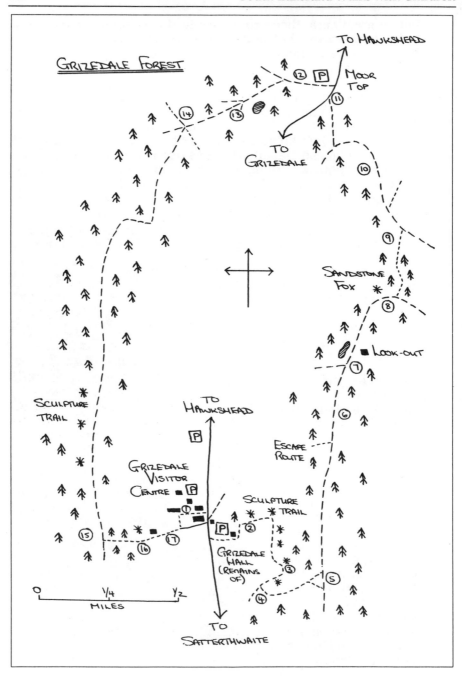

GRIZEDALE FOREST

TO HAWKSHEAD

⑫ P MOOR TOP

⑪

TO GRIZEDALE

⑭   ⑬

⑩

⑨

SANDSTONE FOX ✳

⑧

LOOK-OUT

⑦

SCULPTURE TRAIL

⑥

TO HAWKSHEAD

P

ESCAPE ROUTE

GRIZEDALE VISITOR CENTRE P

SCULPTURE TRAIL

①

P ②

⑮   ⑰   ⑯

GRIZEDALE HALL (REMAINS OF)

③   ⑤

④

0   ¼   ½
MILES

TO SATTERTHWAITE

3. **Pass the shelter & bench on the corner as the path bends around to the left. Cross the suspension bridge over the stream and continue following the blue and white posts.**

😊 The path passes a tree telescope what looks over the campsite. It is made out of a hollowed tree trunk. Look through it and see what you can see.

Many of the trees in this part of the woods are 'conifers' which means they have cones which carry their seeds, and dark green 'needles' instead of leaves. Most types of conifers are 'evergreens', which means they keep their colours all the year round. Not all types are though. If it is autumn keep your eyes open for a tree with needles which is not still green.

4. **Take the steps off to the left, leading uphill and follow the clear pathway the trees.**

(Escape route/pushchair route: Avoid the left turning and continue along the main path. After a short way take the path leading downhill on the right, which will loop round and return you to earlier in the trail. Keep left and return the same way to the visitor centre.)

😊 There are now plants growing on the ground underneath the trees, including rhododendron bushes, blackberries and small heathers. All plants need light to live, so they always grow in the direction of the sunlight, but plants can only grow on the forest floor where the trees are far enough apart. Where the trees are very close together little light can reach the forest floor, so nothing can grow.

5. **After a short way the path bears around to the left. (On the corner there is a bench on the left.) Continue up the steps. Near the top the path splits. Either direction will lead you up to a forest trackway. Bear left.**

😊 This is a working forest, which means that the trees are grown for their wood. Conifers are very fast growing compared to most British trees, and they have tall, straight trunks, which makes them ideal for making 'timber', or planks of wood. Some areas of trees are cut down, or 'felled' and you might see yellow triangular signs warning you to keep away. If you see any forest workers felling the trees, they will probably be wearing 'hard hats' to protect them from falling branches.

When an area has been cleared of trees it is replanted with new trees, which will take twenty or thirty years to grow to their full size, when they will be felled, then the whole process begins again. Look out for areas of young trees. Those which have very recently been planted may have plastic 'protectors' around their trunks, to protect them from wild animals who might otherwise eat their soft bark.

Soon you may notice that there are many trees that are not conifers, they have wide, flat leaves which they lose in the winter. Trees that lose their leaves in winter are called 'deciduous'.

Escape route: There is a shale pathway leading downhill on the left, (this was at one time signed, but the sign seems to have disappeared). Cross the stream and follow the path uphill. Take the stile at the top and keep the wall on your left. After the wall keep with the wire fence to the gate/stone stile and bear left, leading downhill. At the bottom take care while crossing the road back to the visitor centre.

6.   Continue ahead uphill along the main trackway.

☺ Amongst the many different types of trees in the forest there are rowans. These are very easy to spot in the late summer or autumn, as they have clusters of bright red berries, which birds and wild animals can feed on throughout the cold winters when there is little else for them to eat.

Look out for the waterfall on the right and below on the left you may be able to see or hear a stream running in the dip. At certain times of the year you can often see frogs crossing the trackway here, so watch where you step!

Escape route: Take the trackway off to the left, following the posts with white cycles on them. After a short way bear left downhill along a stony footpath. At the bottom cross the road with care.

7.   Continue ahead

☺ Look out for the pond on the left, which you might be able to see through the trees. High up on the right is a 'hide' which is a place for watching birds and wildlife. From the narrow slits in its walls there are views over the forest.

You should soon come across a large stone fox on the left at a bend in the trackway. The fox is carved out of soft red sandstone.

8.   Just after the stone fox bear left along the adjoining trackway, then

The Sandstone Fox, Grizedale Forest

left again along the signed footpath between bracken. The path leads downhill and through a small, dense plantation of mature conifers.

☺ It is quite dark beneath the branches of the conifers. The ground is covered with dead needles that have fallen from the trees. Keep a look out for any fir-cones that may also have fallen.

9. **Go through the large gate and bear left along the trackway, leading slightly uphill.**

☺ You might be able to see Esthwaite Water below in the distance, and in the fields there will probably be sheep and cows grazing.

10. **Go through a gate barring the trackway and continue ahead. At the junction bear right. Follow the trackway down to the lane.**

     Escape route: In an emergency, the quickest way back to the visitor centre is to bear left along the lane.

11. **Join the lane, bearing right for a short way, then left, to the well-signed Moor Top car park.**

12. **Head for the back of the car park and follow the wide trackway that leads into the forest and bear left. (Follow signs showing a blue bicycle). Keep left.**

☺ After some way you should be able to see a small pond on the left, surrounded by grass-like reeds, and with green weed floating on the surface of the water. The trees surrounding the pond, and indeed most of the trees in the forest, are 'conifers'.

13. **After the pond bear left at the junction, leading downhill. (Now following the signs showing a white cycle.)**

☺ There are many streams running through the forest, especially after heavy rain, when all the extra water will drain down from the high land into the valleys below, where it will join larger streams and rivers and will run eventually to the sea.

You might notice on several of the trees there are bird boxes to encourage certain types of bird to nest in the forest and rear their young. The bird boxes have very small holes, so larger birds cannot get inside.

Along the trackway there are many oak trees, from which acorns come. See if you can see any on the ground. There are also several birch trees, which have slim, whitish coloured trunks.

14. **Keep to the main shale trackway, which starts to lead downhill. (Still following signs showing a white cycle.) Avoid the paths leading off to the left, keep with the main track.**

☺ Apart from the many different types of birds that live in the forest there are other wild animals, the most familiar being rabbits and, of course, squirrels, who will feed on the many nuts and seeds that grow on the trees. There are also hares, hedgehogs, mice and bats.

After some way you might notice the first of the many forest sculptures in the trees on the right. This one is called 'Cliff Structure'. See if you can spot it. All the sculptures here are made of natural materials which can be found in and around the forest, such as wood and stone.

(Note: the sculptures are very occasionally removed so those mentioned in the text may no longer be there!)

☺ Look out for the 'Snake Bench' on the left which looks over the valley below towards the white Visitor Centre.

(Notice on the right a post with an 'S' on it. This indicates there is a sculpture at this point which might be out of sight. Follow the narrow winding path uphill through the trees to find 'Midnight Feast': a tortoise with a shell made of rocks. Return to the main path and continue ahead.)

Q: The next sculpture is on the right, and is something that a lot of people are terrified of. What is it?

A: This sculpture is called 'Waiting for Lunch' and it shows a spider and its web.

15. **The trackway crosses a gushing stream, after which bear left along a narrow path, leading downhill. Follow the posts bearing stripes of green, red and yellow.**

(Those with pushchairs: continue ahead along the main track to a junction, and bear left. Follow the track down to the gate and bear right, continuing to the visitor centre from direction 17.)

☺ The rocky path leads quite steeply downhill. Take care where you put your feet! The trees here are mainly conifers again. Half way down the path, on the left, there is another sculpture: a wooden tower. You might be able to hear the sound of people playing on the wooden xylophone near the beginning of the walk.

16. **At the bottom continue ahead, along the farm driveway, passing the farm buildings on the left.**

Q: The road crosses a stream by a stone bridge. What does it say on the bridge?

A: 'Grizedale Hall'.

☺ This is the final stretch of the walk now. If you have done the whole walk, well done. You have probably seen some exciting things and, if the weather was fine, should have had a really good day out.

17. **Cross the stream and continue ahead to the high stone wall. Go through the gate on the left into the grounds of the visitor centre. Continue ahead towards the children's adventure playground, based around an animal/forest theme. Bear right towards the visitor centre**

Grizedale forest checklist

- ☐ A conifer
- ☐ A mountain stream
- ☐ An acorn
- ☐ A mountain bike
- ☐ A giant spider
- ☐ A stone tortoise
- ☐ A tent
- ☐ A xylophone
- ☐ A stone fox
- ☐ A pile of logs
- ☐ A bridge
- ☐ A squirrel

11. Hawkshead & Latterbarrow

Everyone has their own favourite Lakeland viewpoint, and this is mine. A short climb from Hawkshead and there are fine views over Windermere and to the Central Fells. Hawkshead is a tourist hotspot, packed with cafés and gift shops. The town has strong Wordsworth connections, as the poet attended the tiny grammar school here (open to the public), and even stronger Beatrix Potter associations, and here you will find the National Trust's Beatrix Potter Gallery, in what was once her solicitor husband's offices. (Also open to the public). Be warned, at weekends Hawkshead can get packed, so be there early.

Starting Point: Hawkshead village main car park. (NY353981) Well signed.

By Bus: Services from Windermere, Bowness, Ambleside and Coniston

Distance: Just under 4 miles

Terrain: Footpaths and stony trackways for most of the way. A short stretch along a quiet lane.

Maps: OS Outdoor Leisure 7, OS Landranger 96 or 97

Public Toilets: Hawkshead, close to the car park & on the main street

Refreshments: Take your pick. Numerous places in Hawkshead

---

1. From the main car park bear left, then right along the main village street, passing the Tourist Information Centre on the corner. (There are toilets in a short way on the right). Keep straight ahead, passing between the Queen's Head pub and the National Trust shop, and you will come to the Beatrix Potter Gallery on the right. Go through the 'archway' (it's actually square) immediately after the gallery and continue straight ahead through the courtyard.

☺ The ground of this courtyard is cobbled with smooth pebbles. The cottages are mainly painted white and have flowers around the doors and in hanging baskets.

2. Continue to the gate and carefully cross the road. Take the driveway opposite and take the first right turning, signed as a public footpath.

Q: What is the name of the first cottage on the left.

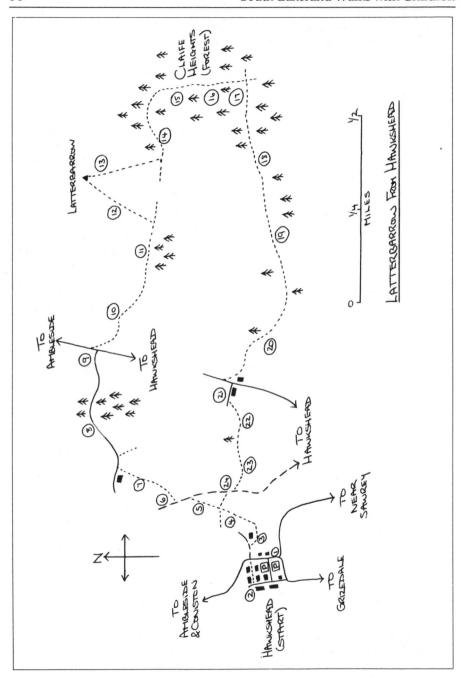

LATTERBARROW FROM HAWKSHEAD

A: 'Black Beck Cottage'. There is a nameplate on the gate. The stream just ahead is called 'Black Beck'.

☺ If you look up to the right, you should be able to see a bare hilltop, which is Latterbarrow, where you're heading. It has a stone monument at the highest point of the hill.

3. **Follow the path past the cottages and cross the small footbridge. Bear left along the bank of the beck for a short way, but then head diagonally right along a well-used path across the field and go through the kissing gate. Bear diagonally right, again along a well-used path.**

☺ This is a grassy meadow, which often has cows grazing in it. In the summer there are many different types of wild flowers growing amongst the grass, some of which you will probably know quite well, like buttercups, dandelions and daisies.

4. **The path crosses over a small stream. Continue straight ahead to a kissing gate. Go through and bear left. Soon you will come to a stile. Cross this and follow the path.**

Q: Next to the stile there is a piece of wood with the word 'lift' on it. What do you think this is for?

A: It is a way through for dogs, so you don't have to carry them over the stile.

☺ On the left there is an area of rushes, which are dark green and pointed at the tip. They can often be found growing where the ground is wet or *marshy,* so if you ever come across rushes like these watch where you're putting your feet, or you might get them wet!

In the distance on the left you might be able to see tents and caravans on a small camping site. Further away, surrounded by trees, see if you can see a large, old house with a tower at one side of it. This is a hotel now.

5. **Go through the gate and bear left along a trackway called Scar House Lane.**

☺ There is a lot of undergrowth at the sides of the trackway, including many colourful plants in the summer, and probably many bees and butterflies hovering around them.

Q: What insect hatches from an egg and eventually turns into a butterfly?

A: A caterpillar.

6. **After a short way go through the gate on the right and follow the path leading uphill, keeping to the edge of the field with the hedge and fence on your right. Climb the next stile (if there is one. The stile and the gate next to it have currently collapsed altogether.) Continue straight ahead.**

☺ There is now a hedgerow on your right, made up of many different plants, including hawthorn which has white blossom in the spring and red berries in the autumn. The hedgerow gives shelter to rabbits and other small animals, keeping them out of the way of larger animals, including humans.

Q: Before long you should be able to see farm buildings ahead. In the middle is the farmhouse. How many chimneys does it have?

A: Two.

7. **Go through a wooden kissing gate on the right and bear left, with the hedgerow now on your left. Avoid the five bar gate off to the left and continue to the kissing gate which leads out onto the lane. Bear right, signed for Latterbarrow. Avoid the footpath off to the right, continue along the lane.**

Escape Route: Take the footpath on the right, which will lead you through Crag Wood. At the other end of the woods pass the first house, then bear right, signed as a public footpath. Continue with Direction 22.

☺ This winding lane has hedgerows on each side, again made up of many different types of plants. Look at all the different shaped leaves; some are oval, some are almost round, some are pointed and some are prickly. There are many different shades of green: from light green, like hawthorn leaves in spring, to very dark green, like holly. Keep well into the side of the lane, and listen for on-coming cars.

Over on the left, over the fields, you should get your first glimpse of the Central Fells, which are quite a bit higher than the fell you're going to climb today. In bad weather when the clouds are low you might not be able to see them at all, or their tops might be hidden from view.

Soon the lane passes through the edge of the woods. The trees here are mainly 'broad-leaved', which means they have wide, flat leaves. They are also 'deciduous', which means they lose their leaves in the autumn.

8. **The lane winds very gradually uphill. At the top bear left.**

    Escape Route: In case of emergency, calamity or desperation for the toilet, bear right along the road, and keep right, which is the easiest way back to Hawkshead.

9. **Continue along the lane for a short way, then take the footpath off to the right. Follow the stony pathway steadily uphill. Several paths bear off to the left, but keep ahead along the main path at all times.**

☺ After a short way, there is a stream down on the left. Notice how the trees all grow along the stream, so they can always get plenty of water.

10. **Scramble up a craggy area and continue ahead, crossing a wooden footbridge. Keep straight upwards.**

☺ After some way, over on the right, you should be able to see a group of trees with 'needles' instead of leaves. These are called 'conifers'. As you can see they are quite different from the broad-leaved trees that you passed in the woods below. If you have ever had a real Christmas tree you will know that they are conifers. The word 'conifer' means 'cone-bearing', as their seeds are carried in cones (fir cones, pine cones) so keep your eyes open for some on the ground, especially in the autumn.

11. **Cross a further stream, after which the path splits. Take the upper path, which soon bears away uphill.**

☺ This is the hardest part of the climb now. It might be steep, but it is only a short way to the top. Growing on both sides of the track is 'bracken' which is a type of fern. In the autumn it turns a rust colour and the leaves and stem die completely, but in the spring new, green shoots will sprout from the ground.

On the left of the path look out for a 'cairn' which is a mound of loose stones. These were built as markers to show walkers the route to the top. It is a tradition for each walker to put a new stone on the top of the cairn, as he or she passes.

12. Follow the wide, well-used footpath between bracken to the monument at the summit of the fell.

☺ As you climb higher between the bracken, a stone monument should come into view, marking the highest point of the fell. If you stand next to it you will see it is probably three or four times taller than you are. You can see the monument from miles around, so have a look for it later, when you get back to the village.

If you spend a few minutes wandering around the flat, grassy top of the fell, you will see that there are good views in all directions. The lake is Windermere, which is the longest lake in the Lake District, and in fact the longest lake in the whole of England, over 10½ miles long. Also there are views over the forest on Claife Heights. As you will notice, some areas have been cut down or 'felled' and might have been replanted with young trees. Nearly all the trees in the forest are conifers.

Things to look for from the top of Latterbarrow: a white house; the turret of a castle; a boat; a radio mast; a farmhouse; cars on the main road; a tractor in a field.

13. Return to the monument. From the path that brought you to the top, bear right and follow the wide grassy path leading gradually downhill between the bracken. The forest should be on your left and Hawkshead down in the valley on your right. At the bottom climb the stile in the corner and follow the pathway through the forest.

Escape Route: Bear right before crossing the stile, signed for Hawkshead. At the bottom the bear left along the lane and continue straight ahead bearing right at the end for the village.

☺ These trees are, of course, conifers. There will probably be dead needles on the floor. Most types of conifer, like pine, fir and spruce, keep their leaves right through the year. In fact, the needles drop off gradually, one by one, and are replaced by new ones, so the tree is never completely bare. However, there are a few types of conifer, such as larch, that are not evergreens. Their needles turn a yellow or brown colour in the autumn and fall off. They will grow back again in the spring.

All plants need sunlight to survive. Where the trees are growing very close together there is little light on the forest floor, so nothing can grow. Where the trees are further apart, more sunlight can reach the ground, so there might be grass, nettles or flowers growing.

This forest is called Claife Heights, and there is an old story about a 'bogle' or goblin who lived in this area, who was banished by a priest to rocks not far from here. Even to this day there are people who claim to have seen a mysterious hooded figure following them along the paths of the forest, so keep a look out for the goblin, and be aware that between the trees there are almost definitely small eyes watching you, and pointed ears listening to you..... but don't worry, they probably belong to one of the many small creatures that live here.

14. **Keep to the main path following the white topped posts. It is very easy to follow and goes on for some way.**

☺ The path might be muddy in places, though stones and logs have been put down in the worst places, so you should be able to cross over without getting your feet wet.

There are many different types of conifers growing in the forest: pine, fir, spruce and larch are all types of conifer. If you look closely you might be able to see that the needles are slightly different, some are dark green, whilst some are almost blue, and the cones also are very different.

In places you can see where trees have been cut down, and stumps have been left and are covered with moss and small plants.

Where there is mud on the path see if you can see any footprints. You will almost certainly see human bootprints, and possible tyre tracks from cycles, but keep a special look out for the prints of wild animals, such as rabbits, squirrels and deer, which roam around freely in the forest, but you will have to be very quiet to see them before they see you.

There are two types of squirrel: red and grey. Red squirrels are quite rare now, though they can be found in conifer forests like these. They are smaller than their grey cousins and have tufty fur on the top of their ears. Grey squirrels can be found almost anywhere, and are very clever at raiding bird tables. They too can sometimes have red in their coats, but they don't have tufty ears.

Q: Do you know what it means if an animal 'hibernates'?

A: It means the animal goes to sleep through the whole of the winter. Squirrels don't actually hibernate, though many people think they do. They are just less active in winter, and will only come out of their nests when they need food. Very wise.

15. **Keep following the white topped posts. After some way the path narrows and passes through an area of bracken. Soon after, it leads slightly uphill over exposed rocks, and there should be a drystone wall on your left. After a short way the path bears left through the collapsed wall and heads downhill in a series of rough steps. Take care on the descent.**

☺ Some areas of the forest are marshy and might have rushes and other water-loving plants and mosses growing on them. Look out also for mushrooms and fungi, which like a damp atmosphere, and might be seen growing on fallen logs or tree-stumps.

16. **Continue along the main path, still following the white topped posts.**

☺ Through the trees on the left you might be able to see an area that has recently been 'felled' or cleared of trees. You may see logs that have been cut down and stacked up, waiting to be taken away. If you do, look at the round ends of the logs and see if you can count the rings. This will tell you how old the tree is. There should be one ring for each year.

17. **The path soon leads uphill. Keep ahead until you come to a meeting of footpaths, where there is a signpost. Bear right, through the gate, signed as a bridleway to Hawkshead.**

☺ Look out for areas of newly planted conifers, which you might recognise as Christmas trees. Conifers are fairly fast-growing, which is why they are grown for their wood, which can be used in building, or 'pulped' to make paper or cardboard.

18. **The path is relatively flat for a way, then begins to lead downhill. Go through the gate and continue along the main trackway. Avoid any other paths leading off in either direction.**

☺ This is a bridleway, so it is open to horses and cycles. On the right is an open area of grass, where there might be sheep grazing.

After some way you might be able to see several tarns through the trees on the left. One of them is quite close, and is covered in summer with water-lilies, which have round leaves which float on the surface of the water, and large white or yellow flowers. In the winter the leaves die, but the plant stays alive in the mud at the bottom of the pond.
Further downhill you will occasionally be able to see Latterbarrow on the right, with the stone monument at the top.

19. **Go through various gates and continue along the main path, still leading downhill.**

☺ After some way the village of Hawkshead should come into view on your left. As well as looking at the scenery around you, try listening to all the different sounds, like sheep or cows, birds or horses, cars or tractors, possibly a plane, a dog barking and people talking.

20. **The path curves gradually around to the right and passes the back of a white house. Go through the five bar gate and bear left along the lane. After a short way bear right along a minor lane.**

Escape Route: Continue along the main lane, keeping right, which is the quickest way to Hawkshead in an emergency.

21. **Take the left turning after the first house (Croft Head), signed as a public footpath, passing the back of the house.**

22. **Go through the five bar gate. Bear diagonally right and cross a stile in a (temporary) fence. Continue diagonally right to a set of steps over a drystone wall. Climb these and bear diagonally left towards the far corner of the field.**

☺ There are several prickly hawthorn bushes in the middle of the field, under which you might find rabbit burrows. Over on the left you should be able to see the lake, Esthwaite Water, and straight ahead is the village. You can probably see the church tower rising above the rooftops.

23. **Towards the corner of the field is another set of steps over a drystone wall. Climb these and follow the clear path as it winds downhill. Go through the gate at the bottom and cross the lane, taking the gate almost opposite, signed for Hawkshead Hall. Follow the well-trodden path.**

Hawkshead Church, with the Central Fells in the distance

☺ Nearly there now .... If the weather has been fine you should have had some good views over Windermere and the surrounding countryside, and might have seen several animals along the way, including sheep, cows, rabbits, squirrels and deer.

24. **Go through the kissing gate and follow the path. This is now the same path as was used at the start of the walk. Continue across the field towards the village. Cross the stream via the bridge and follow the path back to the village.**

Hawkshead & Latterbarrow Checklist

- [ ] A sheep
- [ ] A fir-cone
- [ ] A squirrel
- [ ] A deer
- [ ] A tree stump
- [ ] A fallen log
- [ ] A moss-covered stone
- [ ] A horse
- [ ] White flowers (in spring & summer)
- [ ] Red berries (in autumn & winter)
- [ ] A mountain bike
- [ ] A church tower
- [ ] A plant with prickles
- [ ] The Crier of Claife!!!

12. *Kentmere*

A long walk to the head of the valley, surrounded by impressive high fells.
This is real walking country where the hardy ramblers flock, but this walk
is suitable for those not so hardy as well.

Starting Point: Saint Cuthbert's Church, Kentmere village. (NY456041).
From the A591 Kendal to Windermere road, follow the
signs for Kentmere, passing through Staveley and
continuing along the long and winding road to the end of
the valley. There is limited parking just past the church,
but at busier times a field is set aside as a car-park with
payment by honesty box.

By Bus: Weekends and bank holidays through from Kendal.

Distance: 6 miles

Terrain: Undulating trackways. No severe climbs.

Maps: OS Outdoor Leisure 7, OS Landranger 90

Public Toilets: Staveley, well signed

Refreshments: None in the vicinity

---

1.   **Go through the main gate to the front of the church and bear right
     to a kissing gate in the back of the graveyard.**

☺ This is St Cuthbert's Church, originally built over 130 years ago.
The large tree near the main door is a 'yew'. They can often be
found in graveyards, and were at one time used for building
coffins.

From the front of the church there are views back over the valley,
over flat fields with the River Kent between them. You may be
able to see Kentmere Tarn, which is a nature reserve and not
open to the public.
Once there was a large lake in the valley, called Kent Mere (the
valley is named after this lake) but in 1840 the local farmers had
the lake drained, so that there would be more fields for farming.
This wasn't very successful, as the land was always marshy and
not much use. Many years later the tarn that we see today formed
on the same site.

2. **Go through the kissing gate at the back of the graveyard and bear left along the lane, uphill towards farm buildings.**

Q: Soon on the left there is a stone farmhouse. How many chimneys does it have?

A: Four.

3. **Continue straight ahead along the lane, still uphill. It soon becomes a stony trackway. Keep ahead, passing in front of a barn and white farmhouse.**

☺ Down on your right you might be able to hear running water and see the rooftops and chimneys of the cottages and farmhouses in the village.

4. **Pass a further house and go through the gate barring the trackway. Continue ahead along the lane. Avoid the first path to the left bearing off uphill. Soon after that some rooftops should come into view ahead. Before the buildings take the grassy path off to the left leading uphill between drystone walls. This path leads uphill quite steadily, but not for very far.**

5. **Go through the gate barring the trackway. Avoid gateways on both sides and continue straight ahead, towards the rocky crags.**

☺ Now you should have a good view into the upper part of the Kentmere valley. The middle of the valley is flat and there are probably sheep and cows in the fields. Again, you can see the River Kent, which flows through the town of Kendal and joins the sea at Morecambe Bay.

6. **Keep ahead along the main track which goes down to a farm driveway. Bear right.**

   Escape route: Bear left along the drive and keep left. Once past the farmhouse keep straight ahead along the lane, which curves around to the church.

☺ There is no public road from now on, so the only vehicles you see should belong to farmers or people living in the various farmhouses in the distance. This is a very quiet place which is popular with walkers who can set off from here and head for the high fells that surround the end of the valley. Apart from walkers, you are likely to see many rabbits. If you keep quiet you will

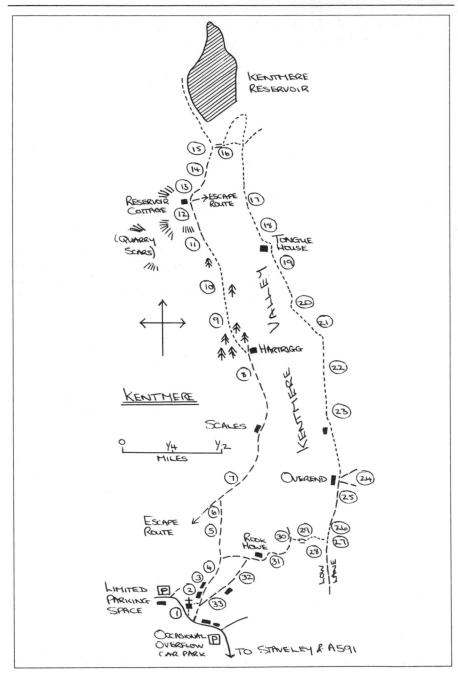

Kentmere Reservoir

15
16
14
13
Reservoir Cottage
12
Escape Route
17
11
18
(Quarry Scars)
Tongue House
19
10
20
21
9
Hartrigg
22
8
23
KENTMERE
Scales
0   ¼   ½
MILES
7
Overend
24
25
Escape Route
6
5
Rook Howe
30   29   26
27
28
4
3
31
Limited Parking Space
2
32
Low
1
33
Occasional Overflow Car Park
TO STAVELEY & A591

KENTMERE VALLEY

probably see lots of them on both sides of the driveway, but they will run for cover when they see or hear you.

Q: The driveway soon drops down towards a white farmhouse. How many chimneys does it have?

A: Only one.

☺ There are many streams in Kentmere. Look out for one which passes under the driveway, and after the barns you should be able to see and hear a waterfall high up on the left, tumbling down the rocks.

7. Keep ahead along the driveway

☺ The valley is now almost completely surrounded by high fells. Notice how there are some trees in the bottom of the valley, but higher up there are none, or very few. If you haven't been noisy you should have seen some of the hundreds of rabbits that live in the area.

Along the driveway there are occasional straggly hawthorn and holly bushes, and many large rocks scattered about.
As you get near the next farm another stream passes under the driveway.

8. After the stream bear left, uphill, along the stony trackway signed as a public footpath, soon leading into an area of trees.

☺ The trees at this side of the woods are mainly sycamores, which have 'keys' or 'helicopters' in the autumn, which are the seeds of the tree. Towards the end of the woods the trees are mainly conifers, which have dark green needles instead of leaves. Look out for fir-cones on the ground.

9. Keep to main stony trackway, now with a drystone wall on your right.

☺ It is more open now, with few trees. Over the wall to the right you might be able to see the path on the far side of the valley, which is the return route. Perhaps there are people walking along it.

Straight ahead you should be able to see the sharp peaks of the high fells. Further along the valley heaps of grey slate should come into view, that have been left over from a quarry, which has now closed down. Look at the path beneath your feet. Some of the stone in the path is slate.

10. **Cross over stream and continue ahead. Go through the wooden kissing gate, after which the track begins to lead downhill. There should still be a drystone wall on your right.**

☺ There is now much more slate underfoot, and straight ahead you should be able to see a white cottage with heaps of discarded slate around it. This is called 'Reservoir Cottage' and you will be passing it shortly.

Soon a gushing stream passes under the track with many trees hanging over it. This is a nice place to rest, paddle or picnic.

11. **Go through the gate and cross over the stream. Continue along the main track.**

☺ On the left is a high rocky fell with 'scree' at the bottom. 'Scree' is loose stones in piles, which have usually crumbled from the rocks of the fells. Also there are very large rocks which have fallen down from the top of the fell.

New trees have been planted in this part of the valley. Trees help to absorb water from marshy ground, and also help to stop soil being washed away by floodwater.
As you walk further along the path look up on your left. You will see that the fell is pyramid-shaped, like an upside-down triangle. Can you see the 'mine' near the top, with slate spilling out of it? A 'mine' is like a cave, except that it is not natural, it has been man-made. Apart from slate quarrying, there was at one time a lot of lead mining in Kentmere. You should never go inside a mine, as they can be very dangerous.

12. **Go through the kissing gate and keep with the main track, passing the white cottage on the left.**

Q: How many chimneys are there on the roof of the white cottage?
A: Two.

13. **The track leads uphill after 'Reservoir Cottage'. Keep left along a path signed: 'no vehicles beyond this point'. There should be a small stream on your right.**

Escape Route: Instead of bearing off to the left after the cottage, continue straight ahead cutting across the valley, though you will have to pick your way across the stream via stones etc. Once across the stream bear right along the main path.

14. Keep to the path, passing a wooden bridge on the right. Continue ahead to the reservoir.

Escape route. Cross the bridge and continue from Direction 16.

☺ The reservoir was built in 1848 to store the water from the River Kent. At the time there were many mills further along the river, and they needed a lot of water, so water from the reservoir could be used in dry weather when the river was low. It is now disused. In the summer the reservoir might be very low, and you might be able to see the mud and stones on the bottom. In June 1996 after a lot of hot weather the reservoir was almost completely empty.

15. Return along the same path, back to the bridge and cross over.

☺ The wooden footbridge crosses the overflow from the reservoir. As you can see, slate 'steps' have been made which will form a waterfall when the reservoir is very full and water runs along this channel.

16. After the bridge either continue straight ahead, cross the stream and bear right along the main path, or if the stream is impassable, follow the well-worn pathway from the bridge, leading to the left, winding along the lower slopes of the dam, cross the river leaving the reservoir and bear right to join the main path, quite narrow and winding in places heading back again along the valley.

☺ There should be a stream down on your right, and you should now be walking in the same direction as it is flowing. You have now passed the furthest part of the walk, and are heading back to the starting point.

Looking over to the other side of the valley, can you see the white cottage that you passed? Or the mine high up on the fell? Or perhaps you can see people on the path towards the reservoir. Soon you should come to more heaps of slate from another old quarry on the left.

17. Keep to the main path which should lead eventually to a ladder stile. Cross over and continue ahead, downhill.

☺ The rocky fell on the left is called 'Tongue Scar'. At the bottom of this there is supposed to be a place where badgers have lived for many years. Badgers are black and grey and live in holes called 'setts'. They are 'nocturnal' animals, which means they usually only come out at night, but if it is early morning or evening you might be lucky enough to see one.

The path now leads down to a stone ruin, once called 'Tongue House'.

18. Go through the gate just before the ruin and follow the stony track.

☺ The doors of the ruin are blocked up with stones to keep people out, as the building is unsafe. There are gates blocking the front of the house, and you can see inside. The roof beams have collapsed and there is no roof left. There is now a tree and other plants growing inside.

19. Pass the ruin and go through the gate on the left. Follow the path with a drystone wall on your right.

☺ The path is getting flatter as it heads further into the valley. You may see horses grazing in the fields, as well as cows and sheep. Amongst the grass there are many wild flowers in the summer, including daisies, dandelions, buttercups and bluebells.

20. Climb the ladder stile and continue ahead along the clear pathway.

☺ After some way the river draws close on the right. As you can see there are many trees growing on its banks, hanging over the water. Look out for the old arched stone bridge crossing the river, but do not cross as this leads onto private land.

21. Continue through the five bar gate and follow the track ahead.

☺ In the distance you should be able to see some of the rooftops and chimneys of Kentmere village, which should tell you that there isn't that much further to go now.

22. Go through another gateway and pass a prefab barn on the right. Continue ahead to a further gate and follow the trackway slightly uphill to the farm buildings.

Q: What is the name of the farmhouse on the right?

A: 'Over End'. The name is chiselled onto a stone outside the farm-house.

23.   **Pass the farmhouse and go through the gate. Continue ahead along the track, passing further buildings on the right.**

24.   **Go through the wooden gate barring the trackway and continue ahead.**

☺ Down below on the right you should be able to see over the flat fields in the valley, with the river Kent running through the middle. Perhaps you can see people walking along the path you walked along earlier on.

The path soon becomes shaded beneath overhanging sycamore trees.

25.   **Go through the gate and continue straight ahead with the drystone wall on your right. Avoid the metal gate off to the right. Continue ahead and cross the stream by a stone slab bridge. Continue along the track.**

☺ On the left is a grassy slope which may have sheep grazing on it.

26.   **Keep straight ahead, crossing another small stream by a stone bridge.**

☺ This is another nice place to paddle, or to stop for a rest or picnic.

27.   **Continue ahead, now with a drystone wall on each side, signed as a public bridleway to Kentmere.**

☺ This is an old cart road called Low Lane. Higher up, out of sight, is another road running in the same direction, called High Lane.

28.   **Go through the gate and continue ahead. After a further gate look out for a series of stone steps in the wall. Climb these and keep straight ahead downhill to the bridge.**

Escape Route: Keep straight ahead along Low Lane, which soon joins a road. Bear right and keep right for the village.

29.   **Cross the bridge and go through the kissing gate.**

☺ The bridge crosses the River Kent. On the right of the bridge the water is quite deep, while on the left there are rapids where the water flows over rocks and stones.

30. **Continue ahead to the gap in the drystone wall. Go through and bear left along the farm trackway. Keep left, with the wall on your left, and avoid all gateways.**

31. **Keep with the main trackway which leads downhill to farm buildings. Go through the gate and along the trackway and pass in front of the farmhouse.**

Q: How many upstairs windows are there in the front of the farmhouse?

A: Three.

32. **Continue straight ahead and follow the main trackway leading downhill, passing Rawe Cottage on the left.**

☺ Soon you should have views to the left over Kentmere village: whitewashed stone cottages and farmhouses. Straight ahead you should again be able to see the water of Kentmere Tarn and

Like I said, Kentmere is a popular place, especially at the weekend!

soon the tower of the church should come into view, which will tell you that this is the end of the walk.

33. Continue ahead to the church/starting point.

Kentmere Checklist

- [ ] A church with a tower
- [ ] A white house
- [ ] A wooden gate
- [ ] A stone ruin
- [ ] A tree with prickles
- [ ] A stone bridge
- [ ] A plant with red berries (in autumn & winter)
- [ ] A square chimney
- [ ] A brown cow
- [ ] A black sheep
- [ ] A rabbit
- [ ] A horse
- [ ] A tractor
- [ ] A white flower (in spring & summer)

13. Near Sawrey

Near Sawrey is situated close to the southern end of Esthwaite Water. It is a pleasant little village of black and white pebble-dashed houses, to which tourists flock throughout the summer months to visit Beatrix Potter's home, Hill Top, and the gentle landscape made famous in her paintings. This walk focuses on the village itself and some of her favourite places close by.

It is perhaps surprising how well the Beatrix Potter Tales still sell, considering most children seem more interested in computer games and the like. Or is it just that grandmas and great aunts buy Potter's Tales because they think that's what children should read? Anyway, this is a nice short walk with enough to keep anyone interested.

Starting Point: Hill Top National Trust Car Park (SD370956). On the right just before the centre of the village if approaching from the Hawkshead direction.

By Bus: 'The Coniston Rambler'; stops include Kendal, Windermere station, Bowness, Ambleside, Hawkshead and Coniston

Distance: 2 miles

Terrain: Possibly muddy in places. Some uphill stretches, but nothing too strenuous.

Maps: OS Outdoor Leisure 7, OS Landranger 97

Public Toilets: Hawkshead, near to the car park

Refreshments: Near Sawrey: pub, tearoom in summer. Hawkshead: cafés, restaurants, pubs

---

1. **From the car park turn left along the lane, passing the large country houses on the outskirts of the village. Keep well into the side of the road and look out for on-coming traffic.**

Q: In a short way there is a playground on the right just before the phone box. Can you find out which year the playground was opened?

A: If you look carefully you should be able to find a plaque, which will tell you that it was opened in 1953. Can you work out how long ago that was?

2. **Bear right along the driveway directly after the playground, passing the phone box on the left. Follow the lane as it winds uphill.**

☺ There are now grassy fields on both sides, which will probably have sheep in them. On sunny days the sheep often lie down in

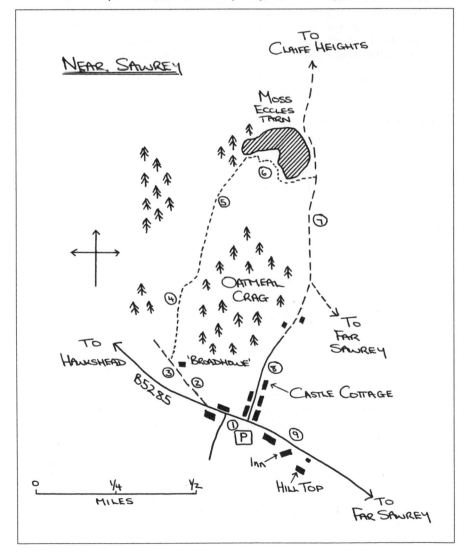

the shade under the trees, where it is cooler. At the sides of the lane there is much undergrowth, including prickly blackberries, stinging nettles, dock leaves and buttercups.

On the left there are several trees which don't have green leaves in the summer. They have dark reddish leaves and are called 'Copper Beeches'. Beech trees have normal green leaves, the same oval shape as those of the copper beech.
As you climb higher up the lane the lake, Esthwaite Water, should come into view down below. There are sixteen proper lakes in the Lake District, and this is one of the smallest ones, but it is still fairly deep, being 80 feet at its deepest point.

3.   **Pass the house on the right, called 'Broadhowe' and go through the wooden gate on the right just after. Note: not the metal gate leading up to Broadhowe, but the wooden gate bearing a National Trust sign, warning that all dogs should be kept on leads. Follow the grassy trackway uphill through the middle of the field.**

☺ High up on the right is a hilltop covered in trees. This is known as Oatmeal Crags, and it was used by Beatrix Potter as the setting for 'The Tale of Mr Tod'. It was one of her favourite places, and she wrote in her diary: "I think one of my pleasantest memories of Esthwaite is sitting on Oatmeal Crag on a Sunday afternoon. . . . "

Q: What type of animal was Mr Tod?

A: A fox. 'Tod' is a northern name for a fox - There are certainly foxes in this area, so you might see one, but it isn't very likely. Although they are quite cat-like, foxes are actually related to dogs. They have red-brown coats and are usually white underneath.

4.   **Pass through the gateway in the drystone wall at the top of the field. Bear right, keeping the drystone wall on your right. Continue uphill (avoid the ladder stile over the wall, which leads onto private land.)**

☺ You might get the occasional view over the lake. In summer there will probably be boats on the water, and on the far shore you might be able to see a boat-house where they are kept.

Q: As you climb higher you should be able to see the trees of

Claife Forest in front of you. These trees are conifers. What does that mean?

A: A conifer is a tree that has needles instead of broad, flat leaves. Look at the next tree you come to. Can you tell whether it is a conifer or a broad leaved tree?

5. **Keep with the wall as it bears to the right and begins to descend to Moss Eccles Tarn, owned by the National Trust. Climb the stile and follow the path through the trees to the right, around the tarn.**

☺ Through the trees on the left is "Moss Eccles Tarn, which was bought by Beatrix and it was she who planted it with the water-lilies, which you should be able to see in the summer, floating on the surface of the water. This was another of her favourite places, where she and her husband would often come rowing on summer evenings. When she died she left this, and much other land to the National Trust.

There are many rhododendron bushes around the tarn. In summer they have masses of lilac flowers. Also keep a look out for fir-cones on the ground. There are many different types in this area. Fir-cones contain the seeds of the fir tree between the hard wooden 'petals'. Squirrels like to eat these seeds, so see if you can see any fir-cones which have been chewed at.

6. **As the ground becomes boggy the path is replaced by a wooden walkway. Pass the gate at the end and follow the wall round to the right and down to a trackway. Bear right, heading downhill.**

☺ This is Stoney Lane where Beatrix often walked, and which features in many of her Tales, including 'Tom Kitten' and 'Samuel Whiskers'. The area of conifers to the right is again Oatmeal Crags. When Beatrix died her ashes were scattered by her head shepherd in 'a secret place' close to Sawrey. Perhaps on Oatmeal Crags, her favourite place from her childhood? Or Moss Eccles Tarn, where she spent many happy hours of her married life? We will probably never know.

7. **Avoid other paths and trackways and keep straight ahead, winding downhill, signed at one point for Near Sawrey.**

☺ To the left is a view downhill over the sort of countryside Beatrix Potter loved: woodlands and walled meadows, and through the

Beatrix Potter's married life was spent here at Castle Cottage

middle of it all is a stream called Wilfin Beck. It was beside it that the characters in 'The Fairy Caravan' camped.

There are many plants along the side of the trackway or growing on the drystone walls, including ivy, ferns, herb robert (which has red stems and pink flowers), yellow poppies and bluebells. If it is spring or summer, see how many you can recognise.
The track soon passes occasional barns and farm buildings. Keep a look out for tractors and other farm machinery. Before long the rooftops of the village should came into view below. The first house on the left, with many tall chimneys, is Castle Cottage, where Beatrix lived after she was married.
On both sides now there are cottages with very colourful, flowery gardens, hanging baskets and window boxes. Most of the houses are made of stone, and many are painted white.

Q: Look at the last cottage on the right? It has something in the wall above the door. Do you know what it is?

A: It is an anvil, which was used by a 'blacksmith' for making horse-shoes.

☺ Notice on the left the white house with the weather vane, which featured as the shop in 'Ginger and Pickles' and was used as Duchess's front garden in 'The Pie and the Patty Pan' .

8. Bear left along the main village street.

Escape Route: The car park is directly opposite.

☺ Notice the post box in the wall, which has the letters GR on the front. This stands for 'George Rex', which means King George. Next to the post box is a stone and pebble building called 'Buckle Yeat', which appeared in several of Beatrix Potter's Tales, including 'The Pie and The Patty Pan', 'Tom Kitten' and 'Pigling Bland'. It is now a guesthouse and tearoom.

Further along on the same side is a pub called the Tower Bank Arms, which featured in 'Jemima Puddleduck'. The inn sign, on the side of the building, shows a scene from the book.

Q: What round object can you see just above the door of the inn?

A: A clock.

☺ A short way past the inn is the entrance to Hill Top, part of a farmhouse, several hundred years old, which Beatrix bought in 1905 with some of the money she earned from her books. She came here for holidays before she was married, when she still lived in London with her rich parents. The house appears in many of her books including Tom Kitten and Jemima Puddleduck.

Hill Top is open from April to October, daily except Thursday and Friday, but do check opening times in case they change. It is run and maintained by the National Trust, who struggle with the sheer number of tourists who flock to visit the tiny cottage, in excess of 70,000 a year, making it the most visited literary house in Lakeland.

☺ From the lay-by opposite the entrance to Hill Top, notice across the meadow the front of Castle Cottage, the large house (probably painted cream or lime green) where Beatrix lived after her marriage, and where she died in 1943.

9. Return the same way through the village to the car park.

Near Sawrey Checklist

☐ A sheep with a black face

☐ A tree with white flowers (in spring or summer)

☐ A rabbit

☐ A duck or swan

☐ A squirrel

☐ A tractor

☐ A person with a dog

☐ A sheep with a white face

☐ A tree with red berries (in autumn or winter)

☐ A radio transmitter

☐ A rowing boat

☐ A plane

☐ A weather-vane

☐ A church tower

Other places of Beatrix Potter interest in Southern Lakeland

Hawkshead: In the village is the National Trust's 'Beatrix Potter Gallery' housed in what was her solicitor husband's offices on Main Street.

Wray Castle: On the western shore of Windermere , a short way from Hawkshead, where the Potter family stayed for the summer of 1882. Now owned by the National Trust. The grounds are open to the public free of charge.

The World of Beatrix Potter: Especially good for that bad Lakeland weather. A multimedia exhibition of everything Beatrix Potter. Displays, visual effects, tearoom and shop. Situated in 'The Old Laundry', Bowness-on-Windermere, only a short walk from the steamer piers. Open all year.

14. Orrest Head

From the viewpoint on Orrest Head, the renowned Lakes writer, the late, great Wainwright took his first glimpse of Lakeland and was hooked for life. It is a short but quite steep climb up to the summit, but well worth it on a clear day. A good introduction to fell walking.

Starting Point: Outside the Windermere Tourist Information Centre, (close to the approach to the railway station) well signed in the town centre. (SD413987)

By Rail: Windermere station, couldn't be simpler. Practically on the doorstep of the T.I.C.

By Bus: Grasmere, Ambleside and Bowness. Bus stops right outside T.I.C.

Distance: A deceptively long 2 miles

Terrain: Mainly tarmac driveway uphill with rocky paths across the summit.

Maps: OS Outdoor Leisure 7, OS Landranger 96 or 97

Public Toilets: None along the route. Toilets available in Windermere town centre

Refreshments: Windermere

---

1. **Directly over the main road from the Tourist Information Centre there are a series of bus stops. Just to the left there is a driveway. Follow the driveway as it winds uphill, keeping left, signed for 'Orrest Head viewpoint'. After a short way there should be a signed footpath off to the left. Avoid this and continue uphill.**

Q: Soon on the left you should pass a large house with its name on the gateposts. What is it called?

A: Orrest House.

☺ The drive curves uphill beneath overhanging trees, rhododendrons and holly. Further ahead there are views to the right over Windermere town, with the lake in the distance.

2. **Pass the back gates of Orrest House and continue ahead, keeping to the main tarmac driveway.**

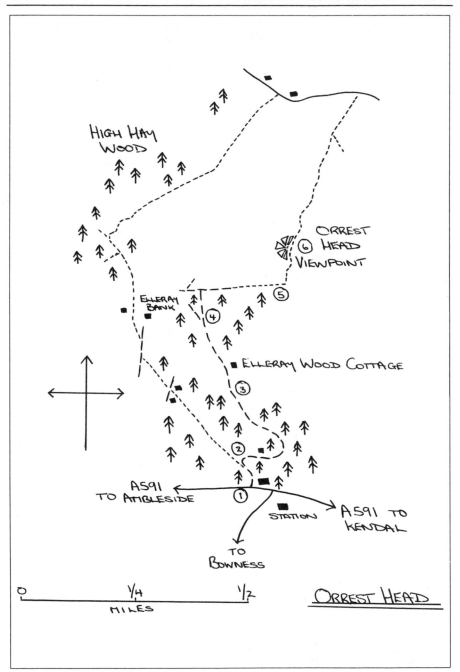

HIGH HAY
WOOD

ORREST
⑥ HEAD
VIEWPOINT

ELLERAY
BANK
④   ⑤

ELLERAY WOOD COTTAGE

③

②

A591
TO AMBLESIDE
①

STATION

A591 TO
KENDAL

TO
BOWNESS

0   ¼   ½
    MILES

ORREST HEAD

☺ Even in the winter there is a lot of greenery along the driveway, as a lot of the trees and bushes are 'evergreens' which means that they do not lose their leaves in the winter. See if you can see any holly, which you probably know quite well. That, of course, is an evergreen, as are 'rhododendrons', which are the bushes with large, oval leaves. In the summer they have many clusters of colourful flowers. If it is autumn or winter, notice though that some of the trees have lost their leaves. See how many different leaves you can find on the ground. Most of the 'deciduous' trees, which do lose their leaves in winter, are beech, silver birch or oak. Can you recognise them?

Q: After some way you should come to a field on your right, where there might be horses, and the rooftop of a house should come into view ahead. What is the name of the house?

A: Elleray Wood Cottage.

3. Continue past Elleray Wood Cottage, at which point the drive becomes a stony trackway.

☺ A short way past the cottage there is a bench on the right. From here there are views between the trees over Windermere lake. In the background, over the water, are the trees of Grizedale Forest. This is a nice place to stop for a rest if you're tired.

4. Follow the main path ahead, which starts to bear around slightly to the right.

☺ Again, on the right, is the field where there might be horses. Notice the gate into the field is made out of two old cart wheels.

Q: What is a young horse called?

A: A 'foal'.

5. Continue uphill between the rhododendrons, signed as a footpath.

☺ Amongst the many types of trees in the woods are evergreen yews, which have red berries in the autumn. See if you can see any. Also there is much more holly here, which also has red berries. Never eat any wild berries or fruits that you come across on your walks. While they might be fine for animals and birds to eat, they might be very harmful to humans. Always look with your eyes, not your fingers.

The path passes several benches, so this is a good place to take a rest or have a picnic before the final climb to the top of the hill. Again there are views over the lake.

6. **The main gravel path now bears around to the right. Avoid the minor path off to the left. Continue slightly uphill, now with a drystone wall close on your left.**

Q: There are several benches here, some of them have names and dates on them. One of them mentions the month of December. See if you can find it. Which year does it also mention?

A: 1972.

7. **At the end go through the kissing gate on the left and follow the main path up to the summit.**

Q: What is the date on the stone near the kissing gate, placed here by the inhabitants of Windermere?

A: 1902.

☺ **(AT THE SUMMIT)** This is the 'summit' or the top of the hill. From here there are good views in all directions, especially over the lake, Windermere, to the high fells in the centre of the Lake District. Perhaps you can see boats or water-skiers on the lake. You should also have a good view of Windermere's many islands. The largest is called 'Belle Isle' which has a house on it which is completely round, and supposed to be the first of its kind in England. In autumn you can clearly see the top of the house above the treetops.

In the other direction you can see the head of Windermere and the high central fells, which are often covered in snow in the winter months. On the other side of the lake there is a castle, Wray Castle. You might be able to make out its towers peering over the trees.

(It was from Orrest Head that the renowned fellwalker and writer, A. Wainwright took his first glimpse of the Lake District, on his first ever holiday. For some years after his death there were plans to erect a monument in his memory, here on the summit of Orrest Head, but after a lot of squabbling with officials it came to nothing, which I'm sure is how Wainwright would prefer it.)

Q: There is a chart at the summit showing the names of all the fells

that are visible from here. How high is the fell called
Wetherlam, which you can see in the distance almost straight
across the lake from here?

A: 762 metres.

6. **Continue straight ahead, passing the viewpoint, and follow the
   well-worn path downhill towards the white farmhouse in the
   distance.**

☺ The path passes two more types of tree which have red berries
in the autumn. They are hawthorn and rowan. Hawthorns are the
ones with sharp thorns.

Look out for rabbits or their burrows, going down into the ground.
You might see a flash of their white tails as they run for cover.
This warns other rabbits that there is danger approaching.

7. **At the bottom bear right, still heading towards the white farmhouse. The path leads downhill to a stone stile over a wall. Cross
   this and follow the well-worn path ahead over the field. (The
   white farmhouse is not in view at this point.)**

☺ There might be cows or sheep in this field. If there are sheep,
look for some strands of wool on the ground. If there are cows,
watch where you step!

Q: What is a young cow called?

A: A calf.

8. **The path becomes a stony trackway leading downhill between
   hawthorn and holly bushes, then runs parallel to a drystone wall
   on the left. (The white farmhouse should again be visible over on
   the left.)**

☺ The wall on your left, and most of the walls in Lakeland are called
'drystone' walls. They get their name quite simply because they
are made of stones piled on top of each other, without them being
held together by cement. The walls are so well made that many
of them are several hundred years old and very rarely need any
repair work. Look at one of the walls and see if you can see how
it is made.

9. **Cross the stone slab bridge close to the wall and continue ahead**

to the stone stile next to the gate. Cross over and bear left along
the lane, soon passing the white farmhouse on the right.

☺ Looking back to your left now, you should be able to see back
along the path you have just walked along. The highest point of
the hill is the viewpoint on Orrest Head. Perhaps you can see
other people up there now, looking at the view over the lake and
mountains.

Q: Look out for the white farmhouse on your right. How many doors
are there in the front of the building?

A: There are two.

10. **Take the first footpath on the left, (opposite the gateway to the
farmyard) keep straight ahead, through a metal gate or gateway.
Note: there are many gates leading in all directions at this point.
Make sure you take the central gate which bars the main pathway.
You should now be heading back towards Orrest Head, with
drystone walls on both sides.**

☺ There may be mud on the path here. See if you can see any
tractor tyreprints or animal hoofprints. See if you can find a
footprint smaller than your own.

11. **As the wall on the left ends continue straight ahead, keeping with
the wall on the right.**

☺ Notice there is a small 'doorway' in the bottom of the wall on the
right. This is called a 'sheephole', and it lets the sheep wander
from field to field.

The path soon begins to lead steeper uphill, and before long the
lake should come into view on the right. After a short way the path
begins to level out, and you may be glad to hear there is no more
serious climbing now!

12. **Avoid the stile leading off towards the woods. Keep straight ahead
with the wall on your right. Go through the open gateway ahead
and continue, now with walled woodlands on your right.**

☺ On the right you should be able to see down into the woods,
where there might be squirrels in the trees looking for nuts or
seeds to eat. Squirrels live in holes in branches, or in a type of

nest made out of sticks, called a 'drey' . If it is autumn or winter, see if you can see any nests or dreys in the treetops.

Straight ahead you should be able to see the lake again. You might be able to see the ferry which crosses from one side of the lake to the other. There has been a ferry crossing near the island for hundreds of years. The ferry today takes cars over as well as people. Perhaps you have been on it.

13. **Continue downhill, with the wall close on your right. Pass an area of loose building stone on the left and continue ahead, quite steeply downhill now.**

☺ If you look up on the left you should be able to see the viewpoint up on Orrest Head, where you were earlier in the walk.

14. **At the end of the field, in an area of tall oaks, there is a series of steps over the wall a short way from the corner. Carefully climb these, which will take you into the woods. There may be no path visible, but make your way straight ahead between the trees.**

☺ The woods are shady, and there are fallen logs covered with moss and fungus. Again look out for squirrels, who will probably be running for cover as you approach. Also in the woods you might see rabbits, mice or foxes, and of course many birds and insects, so look out for spiders hanging from the branches!

Q: How many legs does a spider have?
A: Eight. Insects have six legs, so it isn't actually an insect, but an 'arachnid'.

15. **Keep heading as straight as possible through the trees for a couple of minutes (don't give up hope!) and you should arrive at a clear trackway bordered by drystone walls. Bear left, and soon pass the backs of houses. This soon becomes a narrow walled/fenced pathway. Continue ahead.**

☺ After a short way you might be able to see a vegetable garden over the wall on the right. There might be runner beans, sprouts or cabbages growing in neat rows. If you're tall to see over the wall, can you tell what the different vegetable are?

There are several views of the lake and the roof tops of the town between the trees and houses. Some of the trees are very tall evergreens. (Do you know what an evergreen is?) See if you can spot them.

The drystone walls along this pathway are in shade for a lot of the time, so there are many shade-loving plants growing on them, such as moss, small ferns, herb robert (which has red stems and pink flowers in the summer) and ivy, climbing over the stones with its small suckers.

Soon, very close on the right, you should be able to see the mossy rooftop of a very large old stone house, which looks like the sort of house you might read about in a ghost story.

Q: In a short way look out for the stone gatepost on the left. What is the name of the house on the gatepost?

A: 'Elleray Bank'. The driveway leads up to the house which is hidden in the trees.

16. **Bear right along the driveway of Elleray Bank for a very short way. The path soon continues on the left. Take care not to miss this, as the rest of the driveway is private.**

☺ There are now trees on the left, and on the right is an open field where there are often horses grazing. In the winter they have coats on to help keep them warm.

17. **Cross a further drive and continue ahead along the path.**

Q: Soon you will come to more buildings. What is the name of the flat above the garage to the right of the path?

A: 'North's Point'. There is a name plaque on the front of the building.

18. **Follow the wall on the right. Enter the woods and keep to the path, close to the wall all the way.**

☺ Pass the small stream flowing from the woods and down an iron grid. In very wet weather there might be water flowing right across the whole pathway. There are many mixed trees in the woods here, including oak, yews, sycamore, and beech. Can you tell which are evergreen and which are deciduous?

This is the last section of the walk now. It is only a short way further back to the town centre.

Soon on the left there is a wall of rock, from which stone was once cut, probably to be used for building houses. (Have you noticed that many of the houses here are stone rather than brick or concrete?) Look at the way the trees hang over the edge of the rock, with their roots clinging on to stop the tree from falling over.

19. **At the end of the path bear right along the original driveway, which will take you back again to the town.**

Q: That's the end of the walk now, but one last question. What is the name of the very large hotel that stands on the left of the main road, looking out over the town? It's name is in big white letters across its front.

A: The 'Windermere Hotel'.

Boats on Windermere

Orrest Head Checklist

☐ A bus

☐ Holly

☐ Windermere Lake

☐ A squirrel

☐ A sheep

☐ A round chimney pot

☐ A horse

☐ Red berries

☐ A dog

☐ A person with a camera

☐ A birds nest

☐ A tractor

☐ A rabbit

☐ A yellow flower

☐ A plane

☐ A person with a walking stick

15. Ravenglass & Muncaster

Ravenglass is a sleepy coastal village, and the only one in the National Park. It is very accessible by rail, as the British Rail Coastal Line passes through it, and also, of great interest to children and adults alike, the Ravenglass and Eskdale (Miniature) Railway starts here. Muncaster Castle is a historic stately home with attractive gardens, and is the headquarters of the Owl Breeding and Release Scheme. The views from its terrace are renowned for being amongst the finest views in Lakeland. There is an optional return to Ravenglass on the miniature railway.

Starting Point:	Ravenglass & Eskdale railway station. Well-signed from the A595.
By Rail:	Couldn't be simpler. Ravenglass station on the British Rail Cumbrian Coastal Line.
Distance:	Entire route: 4½ miles
Terrain:	Some small hills, but nothing too serious. Mainly footpaths and trackways, some stretches along a stony beach, and a few short distances along pavements.
Maps:	*OS* Outdoor Leisure 6, OS Landranger 89
Public Toilets:	Ravenglass station & Muncaster Castle
Refreshments:	Ravenglass station & Muncaster Castle

(At the station there are tickets available to all stations along the line, as far as Dalegarth in Eskdale. Also here there are toilets, refreshments, a museum, playground and picnic tables.)

☺ This is the beginning of the Ravenglass & Eskdale Railway, which is the oldest railway of its type in the country. It has miniature trains and carriages, which run from here into Eskdale, several miles inland.

At the end of the platform there is a round 'turn-table'. See if you can spot it. This is for turning the trains round, so they can set off again in the other direction.

1. **Head for the far end of the platform passing the toilets & café on the left. Continue ahead, following signs for 'the Ratty Arms & Ravenglass', up a gravel pathway, passing the children's playground on the left.**

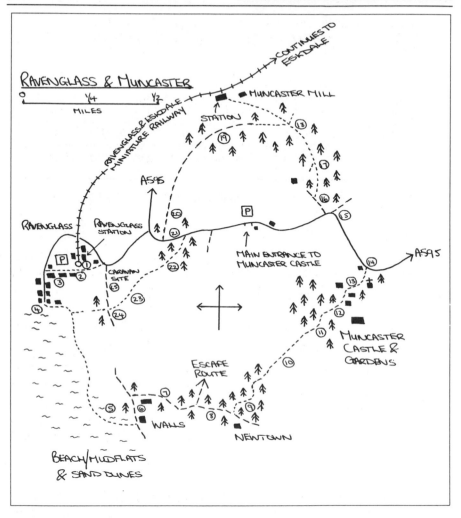

2.   Bear right across the railway bridge.

☺ If you look over the bridge you can see the main railway, which has full-sized trains, not miniature ones. That is the platform over on the right. This railway is threatened with closure, because not enough people use trains these days, even though they are a cleaner way to travel as they cause less pollution. More people have cars now, which cause pollution because of their exhaust fumes.

3. **From the bridge continue straight ahead. There should be a car park on your right and houses on the left. Cross the road and keep straight ahead to the main village street. Bear left.**

☺ Ravenglass was once a busy market town, but today it is a very quiet place, except for tourists, many of whom come on the little railway. This is the main village street, and most of the houses along it are very old, many several hundred years. Some of them have plaques showing when they were built. See if you can see the dates 1898 and 1894. Also, look out on the right and see if you can see an old fashioned petrol pump, standing outside one of the houses.

4. **At the end of the street there is a ramp leading down to the beach. Bear left along the shingle for some way.**

☺ If you look around you there is a lot of sand, and there are dunes in the distance. The dunes are a nature reserve, where Europe's largest flock of black headed gulls live. You will almost certainly see several gulls as you walk along the beach.

Three rivers join the sea here, the Irt, Mite and Esk, all carrying water from high up in the mountains of the Lake District. Ravenglass was once a thriving port, where boats would come and bring goods to sell at the market, but the port is now long since gone, as the river became clogged up with sand, and boats could no longer get here.

5. **After some way follow the ramp off to the left, leading away from the beach to a railway bridge. Pass under the bridge and bear left along the driveway through the trees.**

Q: There should be a large house on the right with many tall chimneys. One of the chimneys has a date on it. What is the date?

A: 1885.

6. **There are various stony tracks leading off to the right. Most of these are driveways to private homes. Bear right along the track with the yellow footpath arrow, signed for 'Newtown Cottage'.**

7. **The track is straight for some way, until passing beneath the pylons, at which point take care to avoid the turning off to the left. Keep with the main path and avoid another trackway off to the right and a further one to the left. Keep straight ahead.**

Escape Route: The last trackway off to the left is a public footpath
(currently unsigned). To make a circular route back to Ravenglass
avoiding the castle follow this through the woods and all the way to the
main road. Here bear left for a short way, and then take the public
footpath off to the left, through the woods. Continue from Direction 22.

8. **Avoid the gateway off to the right and continue ahead for a short
   way. Look out for the gate on the left, (before Newtown Cottage)
   almost hidden in the bushes. Go through and follow the well-worn
   path winding uphill.**

☺ This is a small plantation where there are many conifers (trees
with cones and dark needles instead of leaves) and there may be
other trees in 'protectors' to keep their soft bark safe from
animals who would otherwise gnaw away at it. Look out for
fir-cones on the ground.

9. **Keep to the main path, leading gradually uphill at all times. Avoid
   all other turnings on both sides. At the top of the plantation cross
   the stile and bear diagonally left, slightly uphill, following the
   occasional yellow posts, heading in a roughly north-easterly
   direction.**

☺ You should now be in a grassy field with many prickly thistles,
where there might be cows or sheep grazing. Over to the right
there are views to the bare high fells of the Lake District.

10. **Keep heading uphill until the walled woodland comes into view
    on the opposite side of the field. Look out for the gate (and stile)
    and go through onto the Muncaster Estate, following the main
    path downhill through the woods.**

☺ These are the grounds of Muncaster Castle, once the home of a
very rich and powerful family, who owned much of the
surrounding land. It is now open to the public and is the home of
many large owls, which you might see on your way through the
gardens. There is an Owl Centre here, where owls are bred and
released into the wild.

Many of the plants in the gardens are quite rare in Britain and can
only survive in sheltered conditions such as these; for example,
look out for the tall, thin, cane-like plants. There are many wild
birds in the woods, and several fallen logs which might have
fungus growing on them.

Muncaster Castle

11. Continue downhill along the main path. At the bottom cross over the gravel path and continue straight ahead across the grass towards the buildings.

Q: On the left look out for a fenced area which has tortoises in it. Tortoises have shells which protect them. They can tuck their legs and head inside the shell and will be safe from attack. Can you think of any other animals which have shells to protect them?

A: Snails, which you might see around the gardens, eating plants; crabs, which you might see on the beach; turtles, which are like tortoises, except they can swim, and you aren't likely to see one today!

☺ Also on the left there is a pond with an island in the middle, where there are many waterbirds, including ducks and geese.

12. Bear right along the drive after the pond and bear left before the castellated stables.

(Muncaster Castle is open to the public, but there is an admission charge. The grounds are interesting and offer good views along Eskdale.

In the stables there is a tearoom, which is open to walkers without them having to pay the entrance fee, but it might be advisable to ask first.)

☺ In the background on the right you should be able to see the castle, which, by the way, is supposed to be haunted.....

13. **Keep with the drive, which soon bears around to the left towards the road.**

   (On the right at the bend there are toilets that are available for public use.)

Q: There are bumps on this driveway. What do you think they are for?

A: They are to slow cars down, so that they cannot drive too fast.

☺ On the right in a short way there is a small church with two bells visible on the roof. There are many old graves in the graveyard. See which is the oldest you can find.

14. **Continue to the main gates and bear left, uphill. There is a pavement on the right. Take care crossing the road.**

Q: Can you see the triangular road sign? What do you think it means?

A: It is a warning that the road bends sharply. Most triangular road signs are warnings.

15. **At the sharp corner, where the road bears to the left, take the second footpath on the right, leading straight ahead, signed as a public bridleway for 'Muncaster Mill via Branken Wall'. Follow the dirt trackway downhill towards farm buildings in the distance.**

16. **Look out for five bar gate on the right, signed as a permitted bridleway to Muncaster Mill. Follow the path straight through the woods.**

☺ There are mixed trees in the woods and many types of plants growing between the trees, including prickly blackberries, bracken and rhododendrons, which have large, colourful flowers in the late spring and summer. The flowers attract many insects, such as bees, wasps and butterflies.

17. Keep straight ahead, still signed for the mill, avoiding the uphill path that leads off to the left.

😊 Further into the woods new trees have been planted to replace older trees which may have been cut down. Young trees are called 'saplings'.

The path is a 'bridleway' which means that it can also be used by horses. See if you can see any hoofprints on the ground.

18. At the bottom of the woods the path splits into three. Bear left and follow the grassy path through the trees.

Escape Route/return via the railway: At the junction take the stony middle path, leading quite steeply downhill beneath overhanging trees. At the bottom bear right for a very short way, then left, following the path down to Muncaster Mill. (A water powered mill, open daily throughout the season.) Continue ahead for a short way to the station. Ravenglass is just one stop.

19. Keep to the main path, leading downhill. At the bottom bear left along the rutted dirt trackway. Go through the gate and continue uphill along the clear track.

Muncaster Mill

☺ There are prickly 'gorse' bushes growing on both sides of the path. Watch out, because their thorns are very sharp. In the spring and summer they have yellow flowers which can smell very strongly. Down on the right you might be able to hear cars on the main road.

As you walk further along the path the river 'estuary' should come into view. An 'estuary' is the end of a river's journey, where it joins the sea. You should be able to see it winding away through the sand and into the distance. Also, can you see the main railway line?

20. **Keep to the main trackway, going through several gates until it drops down to the main road. Here bear left along the pavement.**

Escape Route: Bear right along the main road and keep straight ahead for Ravenglass, well-signed.

21. **After a short way bear right along a signed footpath. Keep straight ahead along the winding path between tall trees.**

☺ The trees in the woods are mainly beech and sycamore. Can you tell the difference between them? Beech trees have oval leaves, which turn copper in the autumn. Sycamores have much larger leaves which tend to go yellow in autumn. After a short way there should be a small stream on your left, heading down towards the sea.

22. **At the end of the woods go through the kissing gate and follow the worn grassy path, leading at first straight ahead towards the sea, then bearing diagonally left, leading slightly downhill.**

☺ There may be cows or sheep in this field. Also in the summer there will probably be grasshoppers hidden in the grass making their buzzing, clicking noises. Grasshoppers are insects, and as you might guess from their name, they can jump very long distances. Even if you can hear them they are difficult to see, as they tend to be the same colour as the grass.

As you get towards the bottom of the field you should pass a lone gatepost. There was obviously a wall, fence or hedge along here at one time, but there is no trace of it now.

23. **The pathway leads through a gateway, which bears right along the edge of the field.**

Q: You may be able to see horses over on the right, as there are stables close by. Do you know what a young horse is called?

A: A 'foal'.

24. Go through the five bar gate at the end of the field and bear right along the tarmac driveway, passing the caravan site on your right.

☺ This is the last stretch of the walk now....

25. At the end of the driveway pass through the stone gateposts, then bear immediately left along the footpath, signed for the railway and Ravenglass. Keep straight ahead and you should come to the children's playground on the right. Bear right after this and follow the path back down to the station.

Ravenglass & Muncaster Checklist

☐ A boat with sails

☐ A seagull

☐ A train

☐ A spiders web

☐ A castle

☐ A black and white cow

☐ A duck

☐ A boat with a motor

☐ A pink or red flower

☐ A railway bridge

☐ A nuclear power station!

☐ An owl

☐ A dog

☐ The sea

16. Tarn Hows

Possibly the most visited tourist spot in the whole of the Lakes, and understandably so. Tarn Hows, or 'The Tarns' as they were once known can be seen on countless calendars, postcards, boxes of Lakeland fudge and so forth. It is a busy place throughout the summer, especially at weekends, but is well worth a visit.

Starting Point:	The main National Trust car park, Tarn Hows (SD324995). From the B5285/Hawkshead to Coniston Road follow the signs for Tarn Hows or 'The Tarns'.
Distance:	Entire route 3 miles; Tarn circuit only: just under 2 miles (follow 'Pushchair route')
Terrain:	Undulating stony footpaths
Maps:	OS Outdoor Leisure 7, OS Lake District touring map
Public Toilets:	At one time there were some Portacabin toilets in the car park, still shown on some maps, but they seem to have disappeared. The nearest toilets then are in Hawkshead, near the car park.
Refreshments:	Hawkshead
Pushchairs:	The route around the Tarn is suitable for pushchairs, but the path is a bit bumpy in parts and does rise and fall quite a bit, but never too seriously. Begin at direction 1 and follow instructions for the 'Pushchair route'.

1. **Leave the car park by the pedestrian exit, where there is usually a National Trust warden stationed with his Landrover. Carefully cross the driveway and bear right along the grass, running parallel with the road. This soon joins a surfaced path leading downhill. Keep straight ahead at the bottom and go through the gate. The Tarn should now be on your left.**

☺ This is one of the most popular places in the whole of the Lake District. If you happen to go in a gift shop at any point on your holiday, you might see calendars or boxes of sweets with pictures of Tarn Hows on them, and many different postcards featuring views across the water.

At one time there were three small, swampy tarns here, but a dam was built and the land gradually flooded to form the tarn you can see today.

2. **After some way take the stony pathway off to the right, leading uphill.**

    Pushchair route/tarn circuit only: At this point keep straight ahead along the main path and continue from direction 22.

3. **At the top of the path bear right along the trackway.**

☺ From this path there are excellent views over the tarn, and you should be able to see the two main islands, which are covered with trees. In the distance are the high rocky fells which attract many walkers and climbers to the area.

4. **Continue along the trackway and go through the gate, passing through the disabled parking area to the lane.**

    Escape route: Bear right alongside the lane to return to the car park.

5. **Cross the lane, heading for the footpath sign opposite. Instead of following the arrow ahead, bear immediately left along a well-worn path through the trees with the drystone wall on your left. Cross an access driveway and continue along the stony pathway, still running parallel with the road.**

☺ There are many fallen logs, which have been left to rot. Some might be covered in moss or fungus. Decaying wood like this makes a good home for hundreds of insects that can burrow through the soft bark.

Q: Amongst the many very small creatures you might see in the woods, look out for butterflies, spiders, bees and ladybirds. Which of these has eight legs?

A: Spiders. The others all have six legs.

6. **The path soon leads uphill and comes to a stony trackway, bear right along this, passing through more trees.**

☺ In the distance on the right you might be able to see Coniston Water, and some of the houses in Coniston village. Perhaps there are boats or windsurfers on the lake.

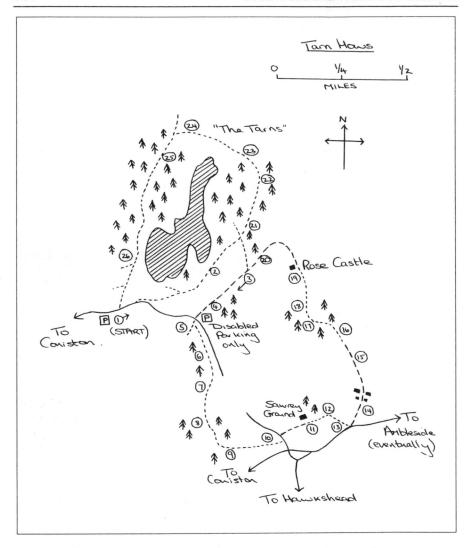

Tarn Hows

MILES

N

"The Tarns"

Rose Castle

To Coniston.

P (1) (START)

Disabled Parking only

Sawrey Ground

To Ambleside (eventually)

To Coniston

To Hawkshead

7.   The path soon winds downhill between bracken and tree stumps. The road is not far away on the left.

☺ You should pass through an area of recently planted trees. Some of them may be surrounded by fences or wire to protect them from wild animals that might gnaw at the soft bark and damage the trees. As the trees grows larger the bark gets thicker and the tree will no longer need protecting in this way.

Tarn Hows

Q: What is a young tree called?

A: A sapling.

8. **The path descends via a set of wooden steps and eventually leads across a small footbridge before winding round to a ladder stile over a drystone wall. Climb this, avoiding the stile to the right, instead bear left across the middle of the field, signed for Hawkshead Hill.**

☺ This is an open grassy field where there will probably be sheep. In the summer there is purple clover growing in the grass. Also there are several prickly hawthorn bushes which have white blossom in the spring and red berries in the autumn.

9. **The path leads gradually downhill, crossing over another ladder stile, and continues ahead downhill. Cross a further ladder stile and bear left along the lane for a short way. Bear right along the driveway to Sawrey Ground.**

Escape route: In the event of an emergency, the quickest way back to the car park is to continue along this lane.

10. Follow the driveway and keep directly ahead between the stone buildings.

Q: The old white farmhouse on the left is now a hotel. How many chimneys does it have?

A: Two. There is also a horseshoe over the door, which is supposed to bring good luck.

11. Keep straight ahead to a stile over a fence after the buildings. Keep straight ahead.

☺ A stream passes underneath the path, and around it there are dark, grassy reeds, which can often be found growing in damp, marshy ground. There are also buttercups and prickly thistles growing in the grass. The purple flower of the thistle, which can be seen between July and September, is the emblem of Scotland, and you might have noticed it on some pound coins.

12. Go through an old five bar gate and keep straight ahead for a short way until you come to a direction sign, then bear right across the open field.

Q: There may be sheep or cows in this field. What is a female sheep called?

A: A ewe. A male is called a ram.

13. Head for the far left corner of the field and go through the gate and bear left along the driveway to Rose How, either crossing the cattle grid or going through the metal kissing gate.

14. Continue along the driveway through the small group of houses and follow it around to the left. It soon becomes a stony trackway leading uphill. Pass the garage on the left, go through the five bar gate and continue ahead along the stony trackway.

☺ The trackway is shaded by overhanging sycamore trees, which have their seeds in clusters of 'keys' or 'helicopters' in the autumn. Sycamores are quite common in towns, along streets or in parks. The high drystone walls on either side of the track are covered with moss, small ferns and other plants that like shade and moisture. The path soon becomes level and a forest should come into view ahead.

15. The path rises slightly to an old metal gate. Go through and continue ahead.

☺ At the gate, if you look around you might be able to see Windermere, which is the largest of the sixteen lakes in the Lake District. It is 10½ miles long, which is three times as far as this walk. You might be able to see boats or windsurfers on the water.

16. Go through a further gate and follow the stony trackway ahead.

☺ Just near the gate there are several beech trees, which have oval leaves and in the autumn they have clusters of 'beech-nuts': prickly casings which have four small nuts inside. Keep your eyes open for squirrels in the branches, or rummaging through the leaves on the ground looking for beech-nuts to eat.

17. Avoid the ladder stile on the right. Continue straight ahead for a very short way, to a stile in a drystone wall on the right. Cross this and follow the path leading slightly uphill. (There should be a drystone wall over on your right).

☺ The path winds gradually uphill over a grassy field where there might be sheep or cows. Over the treetops to your right you might be able to see felltops covered with forests. The bare hill with what looks like a tower on top is near the village of Hawkshead, and is called Latterbarrow.

18. Continue ahead with the drystone wall visible on the right. Eventually the roof of a house should come into view on your left. Continue towards this.

Q: This little stone house is called Rose Castle. It has small arched windows. How many can you count in the front of the building?

A: Four. Two upstairs, Two downstairs.

Rose Castle is owned by the National Trust and is let as holiday accommodation, but has no electricity and no fresh running water. So if you fancy getting right back to nature this could be the place for you.

19. Continue around the side of Rose Castle, passing it on the left. Join the stony driveway which winds around to the left, towards more trees.

☺ Soon the tarn should come back into view with the high fells in the background. As you can see, there are many different types of trees surrounding the water, including copper beech, which has dark red leaves instead of green.

20. **Continue along the pathway, and take the first right turning downhill.**

    Escape route: Continue ahead along the top path. After some way go through the gate, passing through the disabled car park, then bear right along the driveway to the main car park.

21. **Follow the path downhill to a cross-roads of footpaths and bear right along the main path.**

☺ Notice that on some of the trees there are bird boxes, which are put there to encourage certain types of birds to nest here. Also look out for squirrels and rabbits.

22. **Keep to the main path, which soon bears around to the left.**

☺ Many of the trees here are 'conifers', which have cones containing their seeds. They also have needles instead of flat or 'broad' leaves. There are many different types of conifer, including pine, fir, spruce and larch. They are different shades of green and have different needles and cones. Look on the ground and see how many different cones you can find.

23. **After some way, the head of the tarn should come into view on your left. Cross the footbridge and continue ahead.**

Q: Is the steam heading INTO the tarn, or OUT of it?
A: It is flowing INTO the tarn, carrying water from the surrounding fells.

☺ From here you can see the head of the tarn. There are reeds around its edges, and in summer you should be able to see the round rubbery leaves of water-lilies floating on the surface.

24. **Go through the gate and continue along the main path through the trees.**

☺ Again there are many mixed trees, some conifers and some broad-leaved. Many small streams pass under the path and carry water from the surrounding hills into the tarn. At the edge of the water there are lots of little bays and inlets to explore.

25. At the main junction keep left, signed for Coniston and car park.

Q: Amongst the many broad-leaved trees there are sycamore, rowans, beech and birch. One of these types of tree has red berries in the autumn. Do you know which one?

A: Rowan. See if you can spot a rowan tree.

☺ The path is quite hilly as it winds through the trees. After a while you should come to the wide, open area of water at the end of the tarn, where there will probably be ducks, geese or swans. In the spring and early summer you are likely to see the parent birds swimming with their young, which are called ducklings, goslings and cygnets. Be warned, if you try to go too near the baby birds, the parents will peck at you!

26. Go through the gate at the end of the tarn and continue ahead along the path leading uphill, back towards the car park.

Tarn Hows Checklist

☐ A red car
☐ A sheep
☐ A duck
☐ A person with a dog
☐ A white house
☐ A family with a baby
☐ A white flower
☐ A brown cow
☐ A squirrel
☐ A goose or swan
☐ A person with a rucksack
☐ A wooden bridge
☐ A butterfly
☐ A wooden gate

17. Todd Crag

A good introduction to fell walking. A relatively short climb to one of the best viewpoints over Windermere, starting from Rothay Park in Ambleside, where there is a good children's playground.

Starting Point: Rothay Park (NY373044) in Ambleside, behind the Church. Signed from the town centre. There are various car parks in Ambleside.

By Bus: Buses to Ambleside from practically everywhere.

Distance: 2 miles

Terrain: Some climbing, might be wet in places, though some work has been done to improve the paths.

Maps: OS Outdoor Leisure 7, OS Landranger 90

Public Toilets: Rothay Park, Ambleside

Refreshments: The Garden Room Café, Ambleside. Straight through the park and it is facing you at the end of the lane.

---

1. **Entering Rothay Park by the gates near the Church (the toilets are on the immediate left) follow the main tarmac path that cuts straight through the middle of the park, leading to the river. (The children's playground is further along, over on the left).**

2. **Cross the small footbridge over the stream and continue across the arched stone bridge, crossing the River Rothay. Bear right along the lane, cross the cattle grid and follow the road. Go through the gateway on the left, signed as a public bridleway and follow the driveway winding uphill through overhanging trees.**

☺ The driveway is sheltered by overhanging trees, which are mainly beech and lime. Beech leaves are oval, while lime leaves are heart-shaped. See if you can recognise them. On the right is a stream running in a dip. Notice that where the stream is shaded by the trees there is moss covering the stones and rocks, and where the stream is open to the sun there are nettles and flowers that need a lot of light.

This first part of the walk is quite steep, and you might get tired easily. When walking uphill you should take quite large steps and go at your own pace. If you take your time you should make it easily to the top.

Higher up there are good views over some of the grey stone town of Ambleside and some of the high surrounding fells. You might be able to see a large, grey manor house in the trees in the distance. This is Rydal Hall, at one time the home of a rich and powerful family who owned much of the land in this area. Some of the fields near the hall are used for camping. Perhaps you can see some tents amongst the trees.

3. **Continue uphill and follow the drive as it winds past the houses.**

Q: What is the name of the first building on the right?

A: 'Brow Head'. There is a plaque with the name on it near the door.

4. **After the houses the driveway degenerates to a stony trackway. As it bears round to the right, take the stone steps on the left, leading up the drystone wall to a footpath, signed for Clappersgate 1 mile. Follow the path through the trees.**

☺ In the spring there are bluebells in these woods. The bushes with the large oval leaves are called 'rhododendrons' and they have clusters of lilac flowers in the summer. They do not lose their leaves in the winter, so they are known as 'evergreen' shrubs.

5. **Go through the gap in the drystone wall and cross the stream. Take the steps leading uphill.**

☺ Along the stream there are many ferns and other water-loving plants which thrive in the wet conditions. Can you see on the left where new trees have been planted, which may still have their trunks protected by plastic piping to keep wild animals from chewing away the soft bark. These trees are mainly oaks, from which acorns come. This land is very marshy, and the trees have been planted here because they will help to absorb some of the water. Trees and all plants 'drink' through their roots, which can go for some way underground.

6. **After a short way the path splits. Take the right turning, which leads uphill for some way alongside the stream. Keep straight ahead until the path finally bears away from the stream and heads more steeply uphill towards a kissing gate in the drystone wall at the top.**

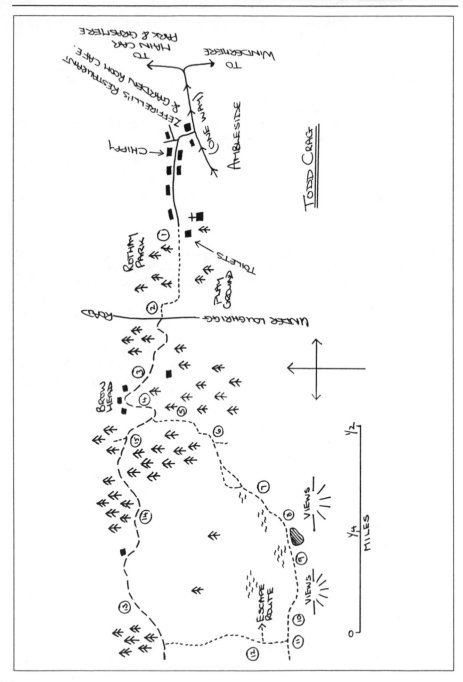

TODD CRAG

TO MAIN CAR
PARK & GRASMERE

TO WINDERMERE

ZEFFIRELLIS RESTAURANT
& GARDEN ROOM CAFE.

(ONE WAY)

← CHIPPY

AMBLESIDE

ROTHAY PARK

①

✝

← TOILETS

PLAY GROUND

②

UNDER LOUGHRIGG

ROAD

③

BROW HEAD

④

⑤

⑥

⑦

⑧

VIEWS

⑨

⑩

⑪

⑫

⑬

⑭

⑮

⑯

VIEWS

← ESCAPE ROUTE

0   ¼   ½
MILES

☺ This fell is covered almost entirely with bracken, which is the fern-like plant on both sides of the path. In the autumn it goes brown and dry, and dies completely, but in the spring new green shoots will appear from under the ground. Look out for sheep who might be grazing amongst the bracken, and take care not to startle them. The grass on the fell is kept short by the sheep.

7. **Go through the kissing gate and follow the main path, keeping straight ahead at all times, (heading in a roughly westerly direction). There should be an area of swamp close on the right.**

☺ Though this is only a small fell, in bad weather the clouds can come down and block everything out, and you won't be able to see where you are going. Weather can change very suddenly in the Lake District, and in any region where there are high mountains. Sometimes people get lost in mist or fog, or have accidents, and the Mountain Rescue team have to go out and find them. You might see the Mountain Rescue helicopter flying overhead, on the look out for walkers and climbers who have got into trouble. If you ever go out for a walk in the countryside by yourself, it's a good idea to let someone know where you're going and how long you'll be, so they can get help if you aren't back in time.

8. **Before long you should come to a small triangular tarn, which you should pass on your left. Keep ahead along the main path at all times.**

☺ This tarn has grassy islands in the middle of it, and reeds and moss around its edges. Just after you have passed it, look back into the distance for views over Windermere. You might be able to see all the islands in the middle of the lake, or one of the many boats on the water. Windermere is the longest lake in England, and is ten and a half miles long.

(There are exceptional views of the lake and surrounding countryside from any of the rocky crags on the far left. If you make a detour to one of them, make sure you return to this main path to continue with the route.)

9. **Keep straight ahead for some way, and you should pass two small tarns. Continue straight ahead.**

☺ On the right is another area of marsh, so make sure you don't go that way by mistake, or you'll end up with wet feet. You might possibly hear loud rumblings, like thunder, coming from the distance. Don't worry, these are explosions from the quarry at Elterwater. A siren should sound before there are any explosions, so you should have some warning.

10. **The path begins to climb slightly, bearing to the left and winding between two crags and coming to join a drystone wall on your left.**

☺ Soon you should be able to see down towards Great Langdale, which is one of the most visited areas of the Lake District, very popular with walkers and climbers. Can you see the River Brathay below? The river often floods in wet weather, and the fields on either side of it end up underwater.

Can you see the white building further away, which is a hotel at Skelwith Bridge. The bridge there is one of the few crossing places over the river, which carries water down from the high fells and empties into the top of Windermere.

11. **The path drops down for some way to a wooden kissing gate. Go through and turn right. Avoid**

Windermere from Todd Crag

the stile off to the right, keep straight ahead, downhill with the drystone wall on your right.

Escape route: (May be muddy after wet weather) Climb the stile and follow the path, keeping the drystone wall in sight on your left. Climb the stile and continue ahead back to the kissing gate and return downhill the same way, back to Ambleside.

12. **Follow the winding path, keeping the drystone wall in sight on the right. After some way bear right through the five bar gate and follow the stony trackway, leading downhill.**

☺ On the left of the path now there should be a plantation of conifers, which are cone-bearing trees, which have thin, dark green needles instead of flat leaves. See if you can see any cones on the ground.

On the right is an area of open bracken moorland, probably with sheep grazing on it. In the distance you should be able to see the higher part of the fell where you walked earlier.
After a short way there should be a drystone wall on your left, which might have moss, ferns or ivy growing on it. Look out for a slate sign pointing the way back to Ambleside. Over on the left now you might be able to see a high mountain called Fairfield. Again, you might see the Mountain Rescue helicopter flying over the fields looking for people in trouble. On sunny days the clouds cast moving shadows on the hills. See if you can see any shadows.

13. **Go through the gate barring the track, and continue downhill.**

Q: You should pass a house on your left. See if you can find out its name.
A: 'Pine Rigg'

☺ Look out for the field on the right, where there are often horses. After a while a stream passes under the trackway, and you can hear it dropping quite a way down into the woods.

14. **Go through the gate and continue ahead.**

☺ There should now be drystone walls on both sides of the track, and also many wild plants, including stinging nettles, dock leaves, bracken and other ferns. Also look out for Herb Robert, which is a small plant with red stems, which has small pink flowers in the spring and summer.

On the right the woods are mainly made up of birch trees, which have slim, white trunks, and diamond-shaped leaves. You might see squirrels running along the branches looking for food. Squirrels live in holes in the trees, or a type of nest they build, which is called a 'drey'.

Q: Soon on the left you should be able to see the rooftops of Ambleside, down below. You might be able to see the church near the park. Does it have a tower or spire?

A: A spire

15. **The trackway will return you to Brow Head. Follow the tarmac driveway back downhill to Under Loughrigg and bear right along the lane at the bottom, back to the bridge and Rothay park.**

Todd Crag Checklist

☐ A fallen log

☐ A horse

☐ A boat on the lake

☐ A stream

☐ A round chimney

☐ A church spire

☐ A sheep

☐ A nettle

☐ An acorn

☐ A person with a dog

☐ Blossom on a tree

☐ An evergreen tree

18. Wasdale Head

Wasdale is one of Lakeland's most dramatic valleys, surrounded by some of the National Park's highest peaks. This walk can easily be split in half, and offers a good introduction to the many faces of the area.

Starting Point: Wasdale Head: The large car park on the right of the road just before the village (NY187085)

By Bus: For some strange reason there is no minibus service through Wasdale. The Tourist Information recommend a taxi from Seascale!

Distance: 3 miles

Terrain: Mainly flat, footpaths and bridleways. A short stretch along a lane.

Maps: OS Outdoor Leisure 6, OS Landranger 89

Public Toilets: Signed from the car park. At the Wasdale Head Inn.

Refreshments: Wasdale Head Inn

1. **From the car park follow the stony trackway away from the road, which leads between drystone walls, signed as a public bridleway to 'Styhead Pass'.**

Q: On the right you should pass a house. How many chimney pots does it have?

A: Five

☺ Straight ahead, the large rocky mountain is Great Gable, which is very popular with mountain climbers. If you've got really good eyes you might be able to see figures on the cliffs. They usually wear bright colours like orange or red, so they can easily be seen.

In a short way on the left is Wasdale Head Church, also known as Saint Olaf's. It is supposed to be one of the smallest, if not THE smallest church in England, and is at least 400 years old, probably much older. It is set in its own graveyard which is surrounded by yew trees. Yews are conifers, which means they have cones, and instead of leaves they have dark needles. They keep their colour all the year round and sometimes have small red berries. See which is the oldest gravestone you can find.

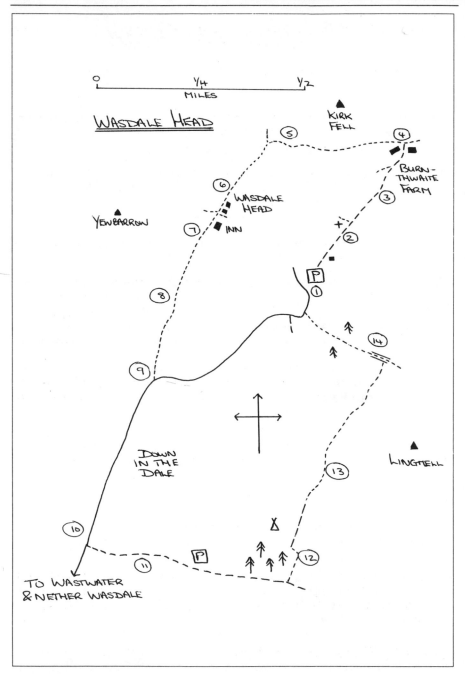

WASDALE HEAD

MILES

KIRK FELL

BURN-THWAITE FARM

WASDALE HEAD

YEWBARROW

INN

P

DOWN IN THE DALE

LINGMELL

TO WASTWATER & NETHER WASDALE

keep their colour all the year round and sometimes have small red berries. See which is the oldest gravestone you can find.

2. **Continue ahead along the trackway.**

☺ Around you there are small walled fields, which will probably have sheep or cows grazing in them. Over on the left you should be able to see the village of Wasdale Head, which is surrounded by some of the highest fells in the Lake District, and in fact in England. The large white building is the inn. The village is very isolated, and has only had electricity since 1979, so there would have been no television here before that!

(Escape route: There are two footpaths on the left, which will lead you across the fields to the village. From there bear left along the lane to return to the car park).

☺ If you look around at the high fells which surround you, you will see that they have only grass and bracken growing on them, but no trees, and nearer to the top there is nothing at all except rock. Trees grow mainly in the valley, where there is plenty of water and they are more protected from the wind, and where there is plenty of soil for their roots.

3. **In a short way you should come to Burnthwaite Farm (National Trust). Follow the track to the left between stone barns. Go through the five bar gate and bear left again.**

☺ The grey building behind you is the farm house. There are often hens running around the farmyard, clucking and pecking at the ground for food, so if you have a dog make sure you keep it on a lead near the farm.

Q: A hen is a female. What is the male called?
A: A cockerel.

4. **Pass the back of the barns on your left and continue between drystone walls close to the stream. Keep with the stream now for some way. The path crosses over several times, and there are many footbridges.**

☺ This stream runs down from Kirk Fell on the right and carries the water towards the lake, Wastwater, which you passed on your way here. Over on the left you might be able to see the rooftops of the village, and might get a glimpse of the lake in the distance.

Further on there are trees along the stream, including rowans, which have bright red berries in the late summer and autumn. Can you see any?

5.   **At the junction (a path joins from the right) keep left.**

☺ Here the stream goes under the path and joins a larger one, Hosedale Beck, which collects water from high up in the mountains. 'Beck' is a local word meaning 'stream'. Again there are many trees along its bank, like rowans and prickly hawthorn and holly.

6.   **Continue ahead, the path is partially cobbled in places. Pass the buildings on the left and keep straight ahead to the old stone bridge.**

(Escape route: Bear left before the bridge, which will take you into Wasdale village. Follow the lane back to the car park).

Over on the left are the buildings of the village, including the pub, which has tables outside.

☺ (At the bridge) This is called a 'packhorse bridge'. The shortest way from one valley to the next was through the mountains, so things were often carried over on horses, who had heavy packs over their backs.

7.   **Cross the bridge carefully and bear left along the beck. Pick your way across the small streamlets that cross the path. There are plenty of small rocks to use as stepping stones. Continue ahead along the well-trodden path. After a short way the path climbs slightly above the beck, but it should remain in sight.**

☺ At certain points there are views ahead over the rest of the valley, and to the left is the head of the valley, where you have already walked earlier on.

8.   **Go through the five bar gate and continue ahead along the path.**

☺ It is often quite marshy in this area, and there are many tall, grass-like reeds growing in the damp soil. There are also prickly gorse bushes. The prickles are very sharp, so don't walk into any

Near Burnthwaite Farm, Wasdale Head, with Great Gable in the background

by accident! Soon an arched stone bridge should come into view ahead.

9.   **Go through the kissing gate and onto the lane. Bear right.**

(Escape route: Bear left across the bridge and follow the lane back to the car park).

☺ The stream, or 'beck' is now below on the left. You can see right over the valley from here, which is known locally as 'Down in the Dale'. At one time there were trees all over the valley, but they were cut down by the people who lived here thousands of years ago to make room for the fields so they could grow crops, and to get wood to build houses or to make fires with. As you can see, there are not many trees left in Wasdale Head, which should be a lesson to us all. There aren't that many areas of trees left in Britain, and we should do whatever we can to stop more areas of woodland being chopped down.

☺ On the left, the rocky fell in the background is Scafell Pike, which is the highest point in England.

10. **Take the footpath off to the left, signed for 'Scafell & Boot'.**

☺ Over on your right you should be able to see the lake, Wastwater, which is the deepest lake in England. It is over 250 feet deep at the deepest point. That's about the same size as a block of flats with 25 floors! The loose rocks that look as though they are sliding into the water are called 'screes'.

This trackway leads over the beck, which empties into the lake. The beck is quite wide here and if there hasn't been much rain there will probably be 'islands' of stones in the middle.

11. **Continue ahead and pass the National Trust car park on the left. After which bear left before the wooden bridge. There should be an area of fenced trees on the left. Keep with the fence and then go through the kissing gate. Bear right and follow the trackway along the edge of the campsite.**

☺ This is a campsite, and usually there are a great many tents here, as it is a very popular area for camping and walking. The tents come in many different, shapes, sizes and colours. Perhaps you have been camping in the past, or perhaps you are on a camping holiday at the moment. It is a lot of fun, but it can get very cold at night!

12. **Continue straight ahead to the end of the site. Climb the stile and continue ahead along the beck. There is a path along the bank for some way, which passes through a drystone wall and continues leading upstream. (In hot weather the beck dries up altogether and you can walk along its bed).**

13. **Keep with the beck and you should eventually come to a stile leading to a wooden bridge. Cross over and continue straight ahead across the field between gorse bushes and surrounding trees.**

☺ Keep an eye open for rabbits and hares darting for cover amongst the prickly gorse bushes. In the distance over on the right you might be able to see the 'INN' sign painted in big black letters on the side of the inn at the village.

This is the last part of the walk now ....

14. **Continue straight ahead to the stile, then bear right along the lane to the car park.**

Wasdale Head Checklist

☐ A gravestone

☐ A tree with berries

☐ A hen

☐ A stone bridge

☐ A white car

☐ A sheep

☐ A birds feather

☐ A bell

☐ A cow

☐ A wooden bridge

☐ Someone walking with a rucksack on

☐ A prickly gorse or holly bush

☐ A rabbit

☐ A person with a walking stick

19. Wastwater & Nether Wasdale

Wastwater is famed for being the most dramatic and mysterious of the sixteen lakes, and not without good reason. Whatever the weather, the screes are awe-inspiring. There are not many (any?) amenities for the tourist, let alone the family, but this short walk passes through some very varied scenery, and the lake shore itself is enough to keep any child satisfied for an hour or two.

Starting Point: Any of the small car parks/lay-by where the road first meets Wastwater. (Around NY151052)

By Bus: As with Wasdale Head, there is no bus service at all through Wasdale. The only option is a taxi from Seascale.

Distance: 3½ miles

Terrain: Footpaths and bridleways, may be muddy in places. No serious uphill stretches.

Maps: OS Outdoor Leisure 6, OS Landranger 89

Public Toilets: The nearest are at Wasdale Head, at the far end of the lake.

Refreshments: Inns at Nether Wasdale and Wasdale Head.

---

1.   **From the car parks overlooking the lake, bear right (heading back towards Nether Wasdale) along the lakeside road or the grass closer to the water's edge if you prefer.**

☺ Wastwater is the deepest lake in the Lake District, and in fact the deepest in England. It is 258 feet at the deepest part. That's about the size of a large block of flats, so as you can imagine, it goes down a long way! No boats are allowed on the lake, but it is popular with divers, who can often been seen with their face masks and tanks of air strapped to their backs, disappearing into the dark water.

Over the lake are the famous Wastwater 'screes' which look like a mountainside of loose rock slipping into the lake. They are often reflected in the still water below. Can you see any walkers on the opposite side, making their way between the many rocks and stones? Or there may be people on the top of the mountain, which is called Illgill Head. Perhaps they are looking down at you!

The screes, Wastwater

Towards the far end of the lake is another popular Lake District view, which often appears on Lakeland calendars and in magazines - the high fells, with their bare, rocky tops. The triangular-shaped one in the middle is called Great Gable, and it is very popular with climbers.

2. As the road beds sharply to the right look for a small path leading off to the left. Follow this down to a ladder stile. Climb over and follow the path through an area of trees and bushes. Keep to the main path, which does not move far from the lake for some way.

☺ On the right you may see some young trees, or 'saplings' in 'protectors' to stop their thin trunks being damaged or eaten by animals. As a tree grows bigger its bark becomes hard and it will no longer need protecting.

In a short way you should be able to see the lake on your left, and you might get a better idea of how high the screes are on the opposite bank. Their height can make you feel very small down here on the ground.

The bushes with dark green, oval leaves are called 'rhododendrons'. (A point for anyone who can spell it!) They do

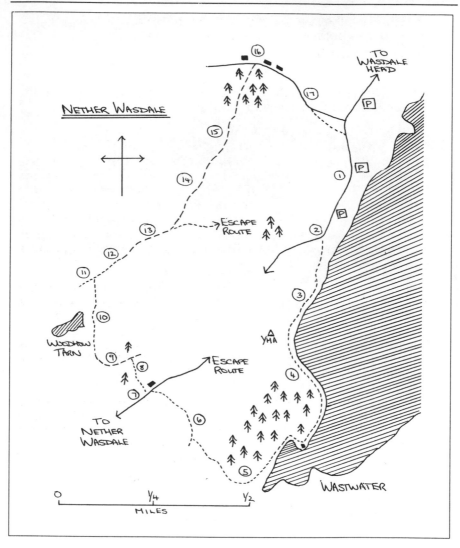

NETHER WASDALE

TO WASDALE HEAD

Escape Route

Escape Route

WOODHOW TARN

TO NETHER WASDALE

YHA

WASTWATER

0   ¼   ½
MILES

not loose their leaves in winter, and in the summer they have lots of large, colourful flowers, usually lilac/purple, pink, red or white.

3. Go through the gate and continue along the shore. Do not bear away from the water.

Q: On the right here is a very large, old house which is now a

'Youth Hostel' where people can stay overnight. It has many tall chimney pots. How many can you count?

A: 16 in all are visible on the main building.

4. Soon after the youth hostel the path bears left, keeping with the lake. Go through the five bar gate and continue.

☺ Many of the trees in this part of the woods are beeches, which have clusters of 'beech nuts' in the autumn, which squirrels like to eat, so keep a look out for squirrels running along the branches. They are very skilful at climbing trees and have sharp claws which help them to keep a grip on the bark and branches. They can leap from tree to tree, and sometimes look as if they are flying, because they can jump so far! Unless you're quiet they will hear you coming and will have darted for cover long before you've seen them.

After some way you should pass a boat-house, where the owner of the big house (before it became a Youth Hostel) would have kept his boat. Through the trees you should be able to see the end of the lake. Water is taken from here and used at Sellafield, the nuclear power station, which is not far away, and which sadly ruins the view from many of the mountain tops in this area, because of its smoking chimneys.

There are several tree stumps, where trees have been chopped down, and there are also many fallen logs which have thick green moss growing on them. Look out also for colourful mushrooms and toadstools growing beneath the trees, but remember never to touch them, as many are very poisonous.

5. Soon the path leaves the lake and continues along a river for a short way, before bearing away through the trees to a gate in a drystone wall. Here bear right, again along the river.

☺ This is the River Irt, which flows out of the lake on its way towards the sea. The field on the right often has sheep in it, or sometimes cows. Can you see the bare tops of the high fells over the treetops?

6. Go through a further gate and continue along the river for some way then bear uphill to a metal kissing gate which opens onto a lane. Bear left.

(Escape route: Bear right along the lane, which will return you in one mile to the Starting Point)

7. **Almost immediately, after the farm driveway, there is a footpath on the right. Head uphill to the gate and continue straight ahead with the wall on your right. The path is signed for 'Buckbarrow & Greendale'.**

☺ This field often has sheep in it, grazing between the large, old trees. If you look at the ground you can see the rock showing through the grass in many places.

8. **As the wall bears to the right keep straight ahead, which will take you down a craggy path to a gate. Bear left along the trackway.**

☺ On the right is an area that is often quite boggy. It is covered with grass-like reeds which are often found in marshy places. Further away there is an area of rocks covered with gorse, heather and ferns. Look out for rabbits and hares running for cover.

You might be pleased to hear that this is about the half way point of the walk.

9. **The track bears around to the right. Go through the gateway/cross the stile and continue ahead.**

☺ Over on the left you may be able to see a small pond, called Woodhow Tarn. All ponds are called 'tarns' in Lakeland. This one is surrounded by reeds, nettles and grasses. It is a popular place for water birds, like ducks and geese, and also a popular place for bird watchers.

10. **Cross the small stream and bear right to the kissing gate, not the five bar gate in the left corner of the field. Continue ahead with the wall and fence on your left.**

11. **As the fence bears to the left, bear right and follow the rough grassy trackway under the oak tree, soon passing the rocky outcrops on the right.**

Q: **(AT THE TREE)** Do you know what kind of tree this is? It is quite common in Britain. If it is autumn you will probably be able to tell, because you will recognise the 'fruit' of the tree.

A: It is an oak, and the fruit are, of course, acorns.

12. Climb the stile next to the gate and continue ahead along the track.

☺ On the right is a rocky area, called 'Ashness How' which has prickly gorse bushes and marram grass growing on it. 'How' is a local word for a small hill, so you may come across it a lot in the area.

The path crosses several small streams, which you will have to stride over, unless you've got your wellies on. Ahead the high mountains should come into view.

13. Keep to the main trackway between gorse bushes. Avoid the track leading off to the left to a five bar gate. Keep straight ahead, passing a conifer plantation over on the right. Soon you should come to a junction of paths. Bear left.

(Escape route: At the junction bear right, signed 'to the Lake'. Follow the path to the lane, then bear left for the staring point).

14. After some way cross the drainage ditch and continue ahead to the ladder stile at the end of the field. Keep straight ahead towards the house.

☺ From here you can see the screes towering over the trees. If you look towards the end of the lake, just after the screes, the tallest mountain is Scafell Pike, which is the highest mountain in England.

15. Again cross several small streams and follow the track through the gate into the woodland. Follow the clear trackway which soon bears to the left and crosses a small stream. Continue ahead through the woods.

☺ This is Roan Wood. It is made up of mixed trees, but mainly sycamore, which you might be familiar with, as they can often be found in parks and gardens. There are many nettles and blackberries in the woods, and also small plants called Herb Robert, which have reddish stems and small pink flowers. Can you see any? Soon you should pass the ruins of a building, which has collapsed and is now covered in moss.

16. At the end of the woods climb the stile or go through the gate onto the lane. Bear right.

☺ This is Greendale. Ahead, you should soon have a view towards the screes, and later the lake will come into view. This is the last stretch of the walk now, and it's all downhill.

Q: Notice the road bridge over the stream. This is called Greendale Bridge. In which year was it built?

A: 1900. It has the date on a plaque in the middle of the bridge, along with the builders name, William Dixon.

(After the houses there is room to walk on the grassy common on both sides of the lane).

☺ There may be sheep grazing amongst the bracken, so try not to startle them.

(Escape route/short cut: Look out for a clear grassy path on the right, leading between bracken. Follow this to the stream then bear left to the road and starting point:

17. Follow the road down to the lake. Bear right for the starting point.

Wastwater & Nether Wasdale Checklist

☐ A cow

☐ A diver

☐ An oak tree

☐ A duck

☐ A sheep

☐ A spider's web

☐ A white flower (in spring or summer)

☐ Red berries (in autumn or winter)

☐ Someone with a rucksack

☐ Someone with a dog

☐ A stone bridge

☐ The highest mountain in England

☐ The deepest lake in England

☐ A white car

☐ A metal gate

20. Witherslack

This is a lesser-known part of the Lake District, and one well worth getting acquainted with. There are miles of quiet footpaths through some of the most attractive countryside in Lakeland, rich in rare British flora and fauna.

Starting Point: A lay-by on the A590. If you are heading from Lindale to Levens, it is just under a mile after the Lindale roundabout, after a Little Chef and petrol station. (SD441826). Alternatively, start from the church at Witherslack. (SD431842) Bear off the A590, along the lane signed for Witherslack. Bear left in Town End, signed for Witherslack church. Follow the lane and you will come to the church on the left. There is limited parking in several small lay-bys after the church. Start from direction 12.

Distance: Entire route: 3 miles

Terrain: Footpaths and trackways through fields and woodland. Some steady uphill stretches.

Maps: OS Landranger 97

Public Toilets: None, except at the Little Chef.

Refreshments: The Derby Arms and adjoining tea room, just off the A590.

1. **From the lay-by on the A590 head 'upstream' for a few yards, towards the petrol station, and bear right along a slip road, which leads gradually away from the main road.**

☺ After a few minutes of walking there should be hawthorn hedges and fields on both sides. The hawthorns have sharp prickles, or thorns, which is how they get their name. In the spring they have white blossom and in the autumn they have bright red berries, which are eaten by birds and other small animals in the winter.

2. **After a short way on the left there is a trackway leading through the trees, signed as a public bridleway to High Fell End. Go through the wooden gate into the Latterbarrow Nature Reserve, owned by the Cumbria Wildlife Trust. Follow the trackway straight ahead.**

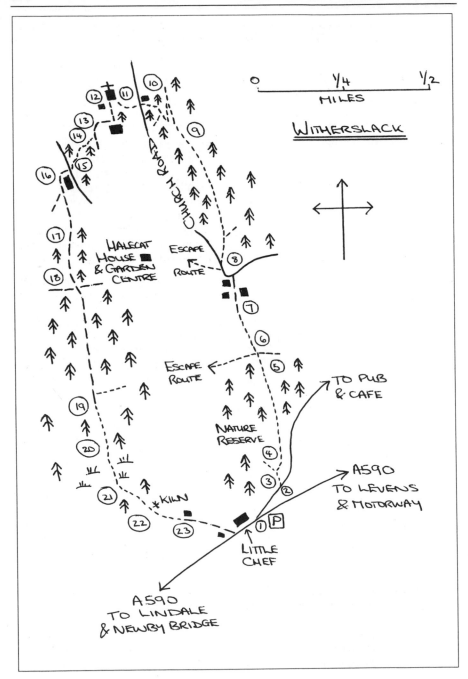

WITHERSLACK

0   ¼   ½
MILES

CHURCH ROAD

HALECAT HOUSE & GARDEN CENTRE

ESCAPE ROUTE

ESCAPE ROUTE

NATURE RESERVE

KILN

TO PUB & CAFE

A590 TO LEVENS & MOTORWAY

LITTLE CHEF

A590 TO LINDALE & NEWBY BRIDGE

☺ This a nature reserve, which is an area set aside for plants and animals, which might be rare or endangered. After a short way on the right there is a notice board telling you about the reserve, and what animals and plants you might see here, including woodpeckers, snails, butterflies and wild strawberries.

Q: In which year was this land purchased by the Cumbria Wildlife Trust?

A: 1985

3. **Straight after the notice board the path splits. Bear right, leading very slightly uphill.**

☺ There are many different types of flowers here in the summer, including buttercups and very large daisies, called 'ox-eye' daisies. There are also many different types of birds.

In places along the path you can see rock showing through the soil and grass. The rock is white and is called 'limestone'. You will see much more of it later on.

4. **Keep to the main path. After a short way the path leads into woodland. It is quite shaded with overhanging trees. There are occasional arrows to show the way. Keep right along the main path. Go through the five bar gate and continue ahead. (This point is the end of the Nature Reserve).**

☺ This path is actually a 'bridleway' which means it can be used by walkers, horses or cyclists. The path is quite easy to follow because horses hooves churn up quite a bit of mud. See if you can see any hoof prints in the mud.

In the autumn, many of the bushes have berries on them, including the familiar blackberry, and blackthorn which, as its name suggests, has long thorns and black berries, and hawthorn, which has thorns and red berries. There is moss growing on many of the lower tree trunks, and also ivy climbing on the trees and rocks.

5. **After some way look out for a crossroads of footpaths, where there is a signpost. The route continues straight ahead.**

Escape route: To cut the walk short and return to the A590 lay-by bear left. Follow the path downhill and across the field, well-signed at this point. Eventually go through the gate into the woods and follow the path leading uphill through the trees. At the top bear left. Avoid a further track off to the left, leading to a gateway. Continue ahead along the narrow path. After a short way bear right along another footpath, signed with a yellow arrow. Cross over the drystone wall via the steps and follow the winding path ahead. Eventually cross over the stile in the fence and bear left along the clear trackway. Continue from direction 19.

☺ In a short way notice the wall on the right, which is made of limestone, and was quarried locally. Limestone is used as a stone for building. It is also ground into a powder and used in cement, or sprinkled on gardens, as it is good for the soil.

Soon on the left there should be a view downhill over the fields, where there may be cows grazing. In the distance there are thick woods, which look very attractive in the autumn, when all the leaves are changing colour.

6. **Continue ahead for a short way, then follow the arrow slightly uphill to the metal gate. Go through and keep straight ahead across the field towards the rooftop of a house.**

☺ As you're climbing the hill, look over to the right and you should be able to see a hilltop with a lot of bare limestone showing at the top. This is Whitbarrow Scar and it is also a Nature Reserve. You can also see the rooftops of Witherslack, and if it is cold weather there will probably be smoke rising from the chimneys. In the distance you might be able to see a quarry, where stone is still cut today.

7. **Go through the five bar gate just to the left of the house and follow the stony driveway. Keep straight ahead, passing various cottages and farm buildings. Avoid all gateways off to either side.**

8. **When the track joins the lane bear left. (Keep to the left of the lane, as there is a wide corner with a partial verge). Avoid the footpath off to the left signed for Slate Hill. Instead take the footpath to the right in a short way, which leads uphill. Avoid the path bearing off to the right, leading to some steps. Keep ahead along the main path, which runs more or less parallel with the lane below.**

Escape route: Bear left, signed for Slate Hill, and follow the footpath downhill. At the bottom pass in front of the stables, after which follow the track to the left. It is well-signed with yellow arrows. Follow the smaller path which bears off to the right, passing in front of a Hall (Halecat House). Keep right until you come to a main trackway. Here bear left. Keep right with the Garden Centre on your right. The track winds slightly uphill for some way through the woods. When you come to the crossroads bear left and continue from direction 19.

☺ The road below is called Church Road, and as you can guess, it leads to a church. There are many different types of tree in the woods, including holly, which you probably know well. Look out for tree stumps left when trees have been cut down. They are left to rot, and are often covered with moss, ferns and other small plants. As the wood decays it becomes soft and makes a home for thousands of insects that easily burrow their way into it to lay their eggs.

Look out for the loose limestone rocks through the trees on the right. You may also see horses or mountain bikers using the path, because again this is a bridleway.

9. **Continue until you come to a cairn made out of limestone rocks. Here follow the path leading off to the left, downhill. Occasional yellow arrows indicate the way. Go down the limestone steps and continue along the path, downhill all the way.**

☺ Notice how there are no plants growing on the ground now, because the branches are very thick overhead and don't let enough light through. All plants need sunlight to grow. Quite a few of the trees in this part of the woods are yews, which have dark needles and red berries. They were at one time very popular for making coffins out of. Not surprisingly there is a church and graveyard very close by.

10. **After a short way the path splits. Bear right, downhill towards the house. Continue through the undergrowth at the bottom.**

11. **Bear right along the lane, and then left to the main gates of the church.**

Q: Look out for the post box in the wall of the church. What are the letters on the front and what do they stand for?

A: The letters are VR, and they stand for Victoria Regina, which is Latin for Queen Victoria, who was on the throne when this post box was made.

12. **Go through the gates into the churchyard.**

The church, Witherslack

☺ The church is grey and has a tower with a clock on it. It was built several hundred years ago. You might notice that there are more yew trees around the edge of graveyard. Apart from being used for coffins, at one time it was believed that they would keep away evil spirits. There are many very old graves in the graveyard. See which is the oldest you can find.

This secluded little church was built in 1664 by order of John Barwick, who was Dean of Saint Paul's and his brother, who was physician to Charles II. The brothers hailed from Witherslack and though they made their fortunes in the big city, they never forgot this pleasant hamlet.

13. Leave the churchyard the same way, by the main gates. Continue straight ahead towards the old vicarage, then bear right along the driveway, signed as a public footpath. Follow the drive around to the left (passing a small car park on the right) and then bear right along the grassy path through the orchard, quite well signed.

☺ The building behind you was once the vicarage, where the vicar of the church would have lived. It is now an expensive hotel. This path passes through an orchard, which is a place where fruit trees grow. Can you tell what fruits are growing on the trees?

They are mainly apples, but there are also some damsons, which are purple plums, often used for making jam or wine.

14. **Pass the tennis courts on the right and follow the winding path down into the woods.**

☺ Many of the trees in the woods are 'ash' which have clusters of seed pods in the autumn, which contain the seeds of the tree. There are also many blackberry bushes and bracken.

15. **At the bottom of the woods go through the iron gate in the ivy-covered stone wall. Go down the steps to the lane, cross over the lane and continue along the stony driveway opposite (Blea Crag) signed as a public footpath to Slate Hill and Cat Crag.**

Q: Look at the house on the left. Can you tell when it was built?
A: 1966. There is a plaque on the side of the house with the date on it.

16. **Continue past the backs of the houses and when the path splits bear left along the grassy track, heading through an area of trees. Go through a kissing gate and continue straight ahead with the walled woods on your left.**

Q: Look around the field. There are many plants growing amongst the grass, including nettles, which can sting you. If you get stung, which plant do you rub on the sting to stop it hurting?
A: A dock leaf. Docks can grow quite tall, and have green 'flowers' at the top. The leaves are usually large and oval.

17. **Keeping straight ahead you should come to another kissing gate. Follow the path straight ahead into the woods.**

☺ The woods are shady with overhanging trees. There are many insects here, such as spiders, moths, wasps and butterflies, and many birds in the tree tops or amongst the undergrowth.

Further on the woods open out and there are many small holly bushes and very tall birch trees, which have small, diamond-shaped leaves and 'catkins', which are like a long, green-yellow hanging fir-cone. There are also more yew trees.

18. **After some way you should come to a crossroads of trackways. Keep straight ahead. The path soon becomes enclosed and grassy**

again, with overhanging trees. After some way there is a stile and footpath off to the left. Avoid this and continue ahead.

☺ In muddy places look for footprints, of people and of animals. There might be rabbits, squirrels, foxes or mice living in the woods.

19. After a short way go through the five bar gate and follow the path through the undergrowth. Avoid the first path off to the right, after which the path curves around to the left. Take the next right turning, so you should be keeping roughly straight ahead. Avoid all other paths off to both sides.

☺ Watch out for nettles, because there are a lot around here. There are also prickly blackberry bushes and many colourful flowers which grow well in the chalky soil. The flowers attract many insects such as butterflies, who lay their eggs on certain plants, so that when the caterpillars hatch they have their favourite food right on hand. Also look out for bees going from flower to flower collecting pollen, from which they make honey to feed their young.

Look out also for mushrooms and fungi, which grow in moist, shady conditions, or on dead, rotting tree trunks. Although some mushrooms are suitable to eat, never pick them in the wild, as some types can be very poisonous. Perhaps, if you are quiet you might see rabbits or squirrels amongst the trees and undergrowth.

20. Keep to the main path which leads through some further woodland, leading eventually to a gap in a drystone wall. Go through and follow the clear path ahead to a stile. Bear diagonally right across the middle of an open field.

Q: There are limestone walls at the edges of the field, and occasional hawthorn bushes, which rabbits often dig their holes beneath. What is a hole called in which a rabbit lives?

A: A burrow

21. Continue straight across the middle of the field, now heading in a south-easterly direction, towards the sound of traffic, slightly uphill.

Q: There are again many flowers growing in the grass, like

dandelions, buttercups and ox-eye daisies. Of these three flowers, which is one is *not* yellow?

A: Daisies; they do have yellow in the middle, but the petals are white.

☺ Over on the right is an area of bracken, which is a type of fern. In the autumn it turns yellow and rust brown and is very colourful. Most plants and trees lose their leaves in the autumn. Those that don't are called 'evergreens'. If you look over to the left you should be able to see some evergreen trees growing in the next field.

22. **Keep straight ahead and avoid the gateways up on the left. Join the rutted farm trackway and continue ahead. This soon curves around to the left, dropping slightly downhill into the trees. Cross the stile and continue straight ahead along the trackway, avoiding the track off to the right.**

☺ After a short way on the left there is a 'lime kiln', which looks a bit like a stone tunnel. A lime kiln is a type of oven which was used at one time for heating chunks of locally quarried limestone, to extract the lime from the stone. Today this would be done in a factory. The arch of this lime kiln is sometimes used for storing hay, to keep it dry from the rain.

23. **Continue ahead and go through the gate barring the track, passing ramshackle farm buildings on the left. Join the farm trackway, keeping straight ahead, which will bring you to the dual carriageway. Bear left, passing a Little Chef and petrol station. There are grass verges to walk on. The car park is literally about one minutes walk.**

Witherslack Checklist

☐ A yellow flower

☐ A blackbird

☐ A wooden gate

☐ A sheep with a black face

☐ A plant or bush with prickles

☐ A squirrel

☐ An evergreen tree

☐ A post box

☐ A white flower

☐ A brown cow

☐ A stone house

☐ A blue car

☐ A butterfly

☐ A spider's web

☐ A church tower

☐ A person walking a dog

50 Questions & Answers for Boring Journeys

Some are difficult, some are unbelievably easy. The answers to all the Lakeland questions are dealt with in more detail within the book.

The Lake District

1. Which famous TV postman (and his cat) live and work in Lakeland?
2. And what is the name of the valley where the stories are set?
3. And while we're on the subject, can you name his cat?
4. The deepest lake in England is in the Lake District. What is it called?
5. Can you name the longest lake?
6. The Queen has a castle in the Lake District. True or false.
7. How many lakes are there altogether in the Lake District?
8. Lakeland is supposed to have the highest rainfall in England. True or false?
9. Can you name the best-selling children's stories set on Coniston Water and Windermere?
10. And can you name the man who wrote them?
11. What was the name of the man who died while trying to break the water speed record?
12. And on which lake did the accident take place?
13. And what was the name of his boat?
14. Which author, famous for her animal stores, lived in the Lake District?
15. Can you name her first published book?
16. Do you know in which village Beatrix lived?
17. What is the name of the highest mountain in Lakeland?
18. There was once a Roman fort at the town of Ambleside. True or False.
19. Can you name the famous poet who lived at Grasmere?
20. Which Lakeland town has a minty sweet named after it?

Cumbrian Dialect

21. What is the local name for a hill or mountain?
22. What is the local name for a pond or small lake?
23. What is a 'beck'?

24. What is a 'force'?
25. What is a 'ghyll' or 'gill'?

Natural History

26. What tree do acorns come from?
27. Which common black and white bird do you often see in pairs?
28. Which tree do conkers come from?
29. What type of insect is a 'cabbage white'?
30. How many legs do insects have?
31. What is a baby swan called?
32. This is quite a hard one. What does it mean if an animal is 'nocturnal'?
33. Is a fox related to a dog or cat?
34. What type of animal lives in a 'warren' or 'burrow'?
35. Some birds 'migrate' in winter. What does this mean?
36. What is a baby duck called?
37. What is an 'evergreen'?
38. What type of animal is a 'golden retriever'?
39. Some animals 'hibernate' in the winter. What does this mean?
40. What is a young horse called?

General Knowledge

41. Which type of fuel causes less pollution: leaded petrol, or unleaded?
42. What is paper made from?
43. What sport is played with an oval ball?
44. What is the name of the street where the Prime Minister lives?
45. What colour are post boxes?
46. What is the capital of England?
47. Can you name the Queen's only daughter?
48. What sweet is made from cocoa beans?
49. In which country is the city of Paris?
50. What do the initials 'U.S.A' stand for?

Answers

1. Postman Pat

2. Greendale, based on Longsleddale, near Kendal.

3. Jess

4. Wastwater

5. Windermere, 10½ miles long

6. False

7. Sixteen lakes, but there are many small tarns

8. True, unfortunately.

9. Swallows & Amazons.

10. Arthur Ransome

11. Donald Campbell

12. Coniston Water

13. Bluebird

14. Beatrix Potter

15. The Tale of Peter Rabbit

16. Near Sawrey

17. Scafell Pike. It's also the highest in England

18. True

19. William Wordsworth

20. Kendal (Kendal Mint Cake)

21. Fell

22. Tarn

23. A stream

24. A waterfall

25. Another name for a stream, usually in a rocky cutting

26. Oak

27. Magpies

28. Horse Chestnut

29. A butterfly

30. Six

31. A cygnet

32. That they only usually come out at night, like badgers

33. A dog

34. A rabbit

35. That they fly away to warmer countries and return again in the spring

36. A duckling

37. A tree that doesn't lose its leaves in the autumn

38. A dog

39. That they go to sleep through the cold weather, and wake up when it gets warmer

40. A foal

41. Unleaded. But diesel is even better.

42. Wood mainly

43. Rugby

44. Downing Street

45. Red

46. London

47. Princess Anne

48. Chocolate

49. France

50. The United States of America

Ideas for Games on Long Journeys

1. If you are in a car you will pass many roadsigns. Children can have a lot of fun guessing what each sign means, and might also retain some helpful knowledge for later in life.

2. Think of a subject, e.g. animals, and each child or member of the party has to say a type of animal. After a few rounds it will get more difficult. If you can't answer you are out. The winner, obviously, is the one remaining at the end.

3. I-Spy, a timeless old favourite. Can make a long journey seem much longer though!

4. Guess who? Think of a famous person, cartoon character etc. and the children have to guess who is it by asking questions, such as: Are you a woman? Are you on television? Give them the odd clue occasionally to help them along.

5. Counting things. On a car journey the most obvious subject would be cars. Each person picks a different coloured car, the winner is the one who has pointed out the most at the end of the journey.

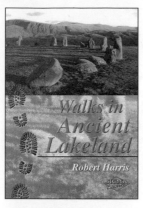

WALKS IN ANCIENT LAKELAND
Robert Harris
A collection of circular walks ranging in length from 2 to 10 miles, each visiting sites and monuments from the Neolithic an Bronze ages, linked where possible with ancient trackways. A walks are accompanied by sketch maps, and the author's intricate hand-drawn sketches. **£6.95**

WALKING THE WAINWRIGHTS
Stuart Marshall
Walks linking all the 214 peaks in the late Alfred Wainwright's seven-volume Pictorial Guide to The Lakeland Fells. Two-colo sketch maps face the descriptive text – so that the book can be carried flat in a standard map case. "An excellent, concise manual on how to tackle the 'Wainwrights' in an intelligent way" – A Harry Griffin MBE. **£7.95**

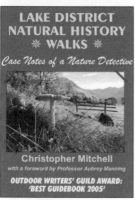

LAKE DISTRICT NATURAL HISTORY WALKS
Christopher Mitchell
Awarded "Best Guidebook 2005" by the Outdoor Writers' Guild! Discover the Lake District's hidden wildlife, geology and archaeology - familiar landscapes in a new light. With 18 walks to choose from, readers can become nature detectives and solve the hidden mysteries. Detailed maps, clear drawings and photographs complement the text. £7.95

THE BLUEBIRD YEARS: Donald Campbell and the Pursuit of Speed
Arthur Knowles with Graham Beech
Fully revised account of Donald Campbell's attempts to raise the world water-speed record in "Bluebird" to 300mph. Includes recovery of the wreck and the funeral of Donald Campbell in 2001. "It's a damn good read and there are plenty of rare photos." – *Focus magazine* **£9.95**

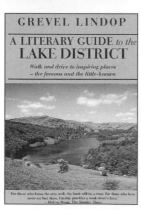

A LITERARY GUIDE TO THE LAKE DISTRICT: Walk and drive to inspiring places – the famous and the little-known
Grevel Lindop
The Lake District's literary connections from earliest times to the present day, illustrated and arranged in five easy-to-follow routes for walkers and drivers. Divided into five very user-friendly areas including the National Park and the Cumbrian coast, the guide is enhanced by specially-drawn maps and archive illustrations. *£9.95*

All of our books are available from your local bookshop and from Amazon.co.uk. In case of difficulty, or to obtain our complete catalogue, please contact:
SIGMA LEISURE, 5 ALTON ROAD, WILMSLOW, CHESHIRE SK9 5DY
Tel/Fax: 01625-531035 **E-mail:** info@sigmapress.co.uk **Web:** www.sigmapress.co.uk